sew
mindful
cross stitch

TWENTY-TWO BEGINNER-FRIENDLY CROSS-STITCH PROJECTS TO BRING YOU COLOUR AND CALM

sew
mindful
cross stitch

TWENTY-TWO BEGINNER-FRIENDLY
CROSS-STITCH PROJECTS TO
BRING YOU COLOUR AND CALM

SOPHIE CRABB

WHITE OWL
AN IMPRINT OF PEN & SWORD BOOKS LTD.
YORKSHIRE – PHILADELPHIA

First published in Great Britain in 2023 by
Pen & Sword WHITE OWL
An imprint of
Pen & Sword Books Ltd
Yorkshire – Philadelphia

ISBN 978 1 39904 587 2

Printed and bound in China by 1010 Printing International Limited

Photography by Sophie Crabb and Amy Louise Photography
Design: SJmagic DESIGN SERVICES, India.

Pen & Sword Books Limited incorporates the imprints of Atlas, Archaeology, Aviation, Discovery, Family History, Fiction, History, Maritime, Military, Military Classics, Politics, Select, Transport, True Crime, Air World, Frontline Publishing, Leo Cooper, Remember When, Seaforth Publishing, The Praetorian Press, Wharncliffe Local History, Wharncliffe Transport, Wharncliffe True Crime and White Owl.

For a complete list of Pen & Sword titles please contact

PEN & SWORD BOOKS LIMITED
George House, Units 12 & 13, Beevor Street, Off Pontefract Road,
Barnsley, South Yorkshire, S71 1HN, England
E-mail: enquiries@pen-and-sword.co.uk
Website: www.pen-and-sword.co.uk

or

PEN AND SWORD BOOKS
1950 Lawrence Rd, Havertown, PA 19083, USA
E-mail: uspen-and-sword@casematepublishers.com
Website: www.penandswordbooks.com

CONTENTS

INTRODUCTION

I often reflect on the reasons why I cross stitch. Among them is my love of crafting, the repetitive and simple nature of slow stitching and the creative joy you experience when a piece comes to life in front of your eyes. But above all, my love for cross stitch stems from a position of well-being and mindfulness.

Over the years cross stitch has become a very important part of my life and is imperative to my mental well-being when I find my mood deteriorating. This particular craft gives my mental health a profound and positive boost, and after speaking with several other cross stitchers, it is clear that I am not alone. But why? Why does crafting, cross stitch in particular, have such a big impact on our wellness?

I write this book not as a mental health expert, nor as someone with a perfect bill of mental wellness. Neither am I here to share profound secrets that will change your life – instead I write this to share some honesty about my own experiences of depression and, more specifically, why cross stitch holds a very special place in my wellness journey.

Over the past few months, I have been lucky enough to speak with other crafters who have shared similar wellness journeys. Each person I have spoken to has been open and honest with their story and I am very grateful to them all. These conversations have taught me more than I ever expected. What started as a research questionnaire to gain clarity on the topic I wanted to cover, turned into vulnerable conversations about our well-being and the emotive reasons behind our need to stitch. I have spoken to fellow crafters who have used cross stitch to channel feelings of grief, anxiety, obsessive body image and family trauma. Topics that I know will have been very difficult to be honest about. These conversations have taught me a lot about the benefits of stitching and that it is so much more than a relaxing craft for so many people.

Combining research, my own experiences, and these honest conversations, I bring you a collection of cross-stitch projects each of which holds a very personal message. Through these twenty-two projects I will share how I have overcome my own mental battles and why we should focus more on the things that really matter in life.

I hope that through the pages of this book you will find new ways to calm your mind while creating colourful cross stitch pieces to fill your home with joy.

ABOUT SOPHIE

Before we delve in, let me introduce myself properly. I'm Sophie. I am a wife, mum, daughter, sister, small-business owner and recently turned author. I often describe myself as a cross-stitch enthusiast and it's because I am exactly that, very enthusiastic about my love of cross stitch.

Born in Norfolk, I love country life. I love long walks in the woods, afternoons in a pub garden and, yes, you guessed it, a lot of crafting. I have always been a crafter - even from a young age. Being creative with my brain comes relatively easy to me and you can often find me making, creating, DIYing and generally seeing what I can add to my to-do list next.

I first picked up cross stitch on a regular trip to my local craft store, while searching for my next project to tackle. At the time I was in what I'd call a mental health rut and struggling to remain in control of my emotions - more commonly known as depression. That first cross-stitch project helped me to focus my attention away from my overthinking mind and into a place of relaxation. I slowly regained control over my emotions, and I truly believe that my little pink flamingo cross stitch kick-started my journey back to wellness.

Fast forward to 2019, and shortly after my now 4-year-old was born, I found myself searching for the independence and freedom you don't always find within a traditional nine to five job. That creative side of my brain (the right hemisphere to be precise) was eagerly waiting to be engaged and from a Sunday afternoon idea on the sofa, Sew Sophie Crafts was born.

Sew Sophie Crafts is where my passion and hobby became a business dream. As a small business owner I design, create, pack and make cross stitch kits for beginners. Each kit is designed to give you a mindful escape when life gets busy, and I hope you'll see that theme reflected across the pages of this book.

Cross stitch has played such an influential role in my well-being journey, and I love being able to share the mindful benefits of it with other craft lovers like me. Never could I have imagined the business I set up from a desk in the corner of our living room would turn into my full-time job.

I'll delve more into my own experiences of depression and crafting for calm through the pages of this book, and I hope you'll read on to discover how I have personally used cross stitch to build a safe space within my mind.

WHAT DOES IT MEAN TO BE MINDFUL?

You'll hear me mention mindfulness quite a lot over the course of these pages. You might be familiar with the concept, or perhaps it's something you've heard about but not quite understood the meaning of. So what is it?

Originating from Buddhist culture, mindfulness is a practised state of mind. In short, being mindful is to live fully in every moment. To accept, acknowledge and be non-judgmental of your thoughts.

You don't have to be an expert; mindfulness can in fact be practised by anyone, anywhere and is essentially the opposite of running in 'autopilot'.

Mindfulness can be practised in a number of ways, more commonly you'll see it linked with meditation. The concept is very simple, but it does take practice. I write this as someone who is still practising, but very much enjoying the journey and where it is taking me.

Mindfulness aims to help you:

- become more self-aware
- feel calmer and less stressed
- feel more able to choose how to respond to your thoughts and feelings
- cope with difficult or unhelpful thoughts
- be kinder towards yourself

© Mind. This information is published in full at mind.org.uk

TOOLS AND MATERIALS

Embroidery Thread

For each of the projects in this book I have used DMC branded embroidery thread. It is one of the best-known brands and is available in most craft or haberdashery stores. DMC is also the brand of thread I use in all of my cross-stitch kits, so if you have already stitched one of my kits or patterns, you're likely to be familiar with the brand.

Embroidery thread is available to buy in skeins, which are 8m in length and consist of six strands of thread wound together. For traditional cross stitch you will use two strands of thread, so it is important to separate these strands before you begin stitching (more on this in the How to Cross Stitch section).

Each project in the book requires no more than one skein of thread in each colour.

Aida

Aida is a gridded fabric; it is specific to cross stitching and is available in a variety of counts. Each of the projects in this book use 14 count aida, which means there are fourteen squares (or stitches) per inch of fabric. This is a very common fabric count for beginner-friendly cross-stitch patterns.

TIP

Experiment with different aida counts to see how the designs differ:
- Try a larger count fabric to make your stitching smaller.
- Use a smaller count of aida to make your finished stitching larger.

My favourite brand of aida is Zweigart which is a German-manufactured material.

I chose white fabric for each of the projects in this book; however, there are many different colour variations of aida so experiment with your own thread and aida combinations as you see fit.

Needles

You'll also need a specific cross stitch needle. For 14 count aida I would recommend a size 24 embroidery/tapestry needle which will glide easily through the holes in your fabric. This size needle is fairly blunt in comparison to a normal sewing needle and will also have a larger eye for threading.

Embroidery Hoop

Within this book there are projects suitable for various hoop sizes, ranging from 3-inch to 6-inch. There are also some small oval hoops used.

The hoop has two main purposes:

1. To hold your fabric securely while you stitch, making it easier to count and follow the squares on your fabric.

2. To display your work. You can use the hoop as a frame and hang it directly on your wall or on a mini stand/easel.

The use of a hoop is optional and does come down to personal preference. You may prefer to stitch with the fabric in your hand rather than stretched in a hoop. I enjoy using a wooden Whitecroft brand hoop; you can also purchase bamboo, beechwood or plastic embroidery hoops from general haberdashery stores.

Scissors

Any scissors will work. Yes, even the kitchen scissors will do the job. Embroidery scissors are ideal because they are small, precise and handy to keep with your project. They are usually sharper too, so they can snip through thread ends neatly.

Needle Minder

This is not a necessity for stitching, but it is a very handy tool. A needle minder is used to hold your needle securely while you're not using it. For example, it can be very useful while you change threads or take a sip of tea (or wine).

The needle minder will consist of two magnets. One that goes on the front of your fabric and the other on the back to hold it securely. Place your needle on to the front of the needle minder when necessary and avoid the need to poke it through your fabric or into the arm of your sofa.

Snap Frame

Most of my projects have been stitched in a hoop; however, an alternative to this is a snap frame (see project Take a Moment to Meditate, in Self-Care Stitches).

The snap frame works in a similar way to the embroidery hoop to hold your fabric securely while stitching. The added benefit of working on a frame is that it doesn't leave creases on your fabric the same way a hoop often does. If you are intending to frame a project rather than displaying it in the hoop, I would recommend trying a snap frame to avoid having to iron hoop creases out of your fabric.

CHAPTER ONE

GETTING STARTED WITH CROSS STITCH

Whether you're new to cross stitch or reading this section to refresh your memory, here are some simple step-by-step instructions to guide you through the main cross stitch techniques with some handy tips thrown in too.

HOW TO READ A CROSS-STITCH PATTERN

Your cross-stitch pattern will be shown in a grid, with many of the squares containing small, coloured symbols.

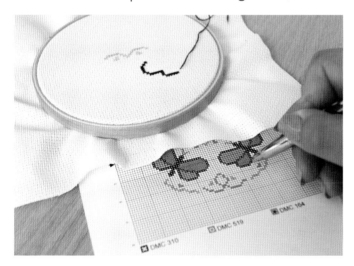
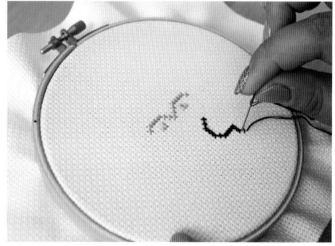

Each of the symbols on your pattern will become a cross on your fabric, with the varying symbols representing the different shades of thread to use for that particular cross.

Your aida fabric is gridded in a similar way to your pattern so you will be copying the pattern on to your fabric, one cross at a time.

TIP Start stitching from the centre of your fabric. The red lines on your pattern will help you determine the stitches closest to the centre of your pattern. This ensures that your stitching will be fairly central to your piece of fabric.

In this example (Exactly Where I Need to Be, in Positive Affirmations) I have started the project by stitching the blue and green shades in the centre of the hoop, before counting down to the black of the butterfly wings.

One of the easiest ways to start cross stitching is to work through one colour of thread at a time, counting the stitches required and copying this across on to your fabric.

USING AN EMBROIDERY HOOP

1. You may wish to use an embroidery hoop while stitching. The hoop will be made up of two pieces of wood (or plastic): an inner and outer hoop.

2. To separate the hoops, loosen the screw at the top of your embroidery hoop. This will allow you to remove the inner hoop.

3. Place the inner hoop on a flat surface and lay your aida fabric over the top.

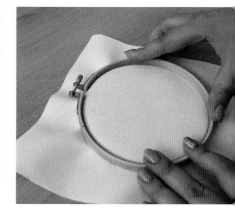

4. Place your outer hoop on top of the fabric and push down on to the inner hoop.

5. This will sandwich your fabric between the two pieces of wood to hold it securely in place. Tighten the screw at the top of your hoop, pulling the fabric gently around the edges so it remains tight (similar to a drum skin).

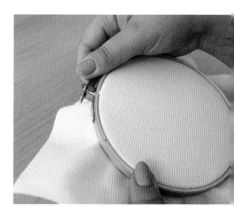

USING A SNAP FRAME

An alternative to using an embroidery hoop is a snap frame. These come in multiple sizes and can be used to hold your fabric securely without leaving hoop creases.

The frame will include four clips, start by removing these as pictured.

1. Lay your fabric over the frame and wrap it around two of the frame sides.

2. Snap the clips back on to the frame over your fabric, to hold it in place. Fold the two remaining sides of fabric over the frame and secure with the final clips

3. Your fabric is now securely in place on the frame, ready to begin stitching.

STARTING A NEW THREAD

Most cross-stitch patterns that use 14 count aida (and all of the projects in this book) suggest using two strands of thread on your needle to stitch each of your crosses. Where two strands of thread are required, I use the 'Loop Method' which is one of the quickest and easiest ways to start a new thread.

TIP If using skeins of DMC thread, pull the thread from the loose end by the barcoded sticker. This avoids any unnecessary tangling.

Cut your length of thread. To do this, hold the end of thread between your fingertips and run the length to the top of your shoulder. This is often the perfect length of thread and is a great way to quickly measure and cut without needing a tape measure. It also avoids cutting thread too long and getting yourself in a tangle.

Your embroidery thread is made up of six strands. To begin with you'll need to remove one single strand from the group of six. To do this, hold the six strands between your thumb and index finger. Pull a single strand with your other hand in one smooth motion. The remaining strands will bunch up as you do this, however as the single strand is removed, the bunch will then release.

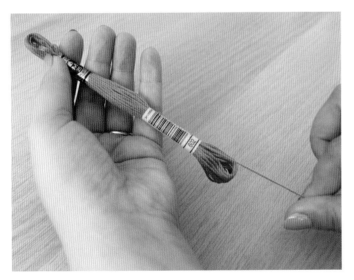
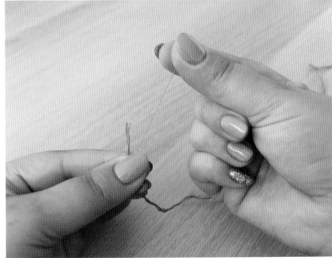

The Loop Method

1. Fold your single strand in half and thread this on to your needle where the two ends meet.

2. Locate where you will be starting your first cross, then pass the needle from the back of your fabric to the front, through the hole to the bottom left of where your first cross will be.

3. Leave the loop end of your thread behind, at the back of your fabric.

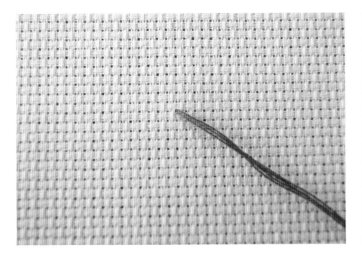
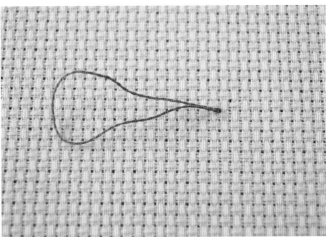

4. On the front of your fabric, pass your needle back through the hole to the top right of your cross.

Front View

Back View

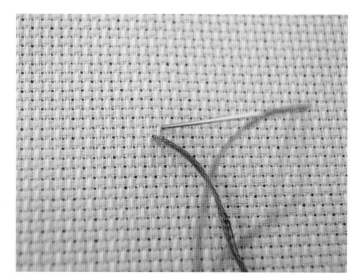

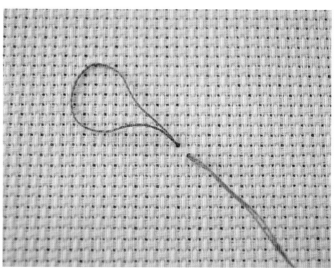

5. Pass your needle through the loop you left at the back of your fabric, then pull to secure.

Back View

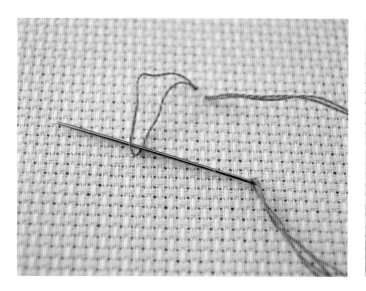

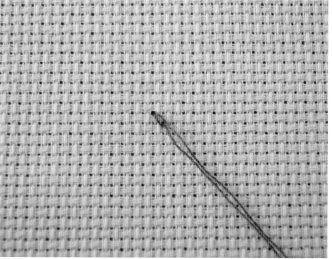

6. To continue this first cross, push your needle back through your aida to the bottom right corner of your cross.

Front View

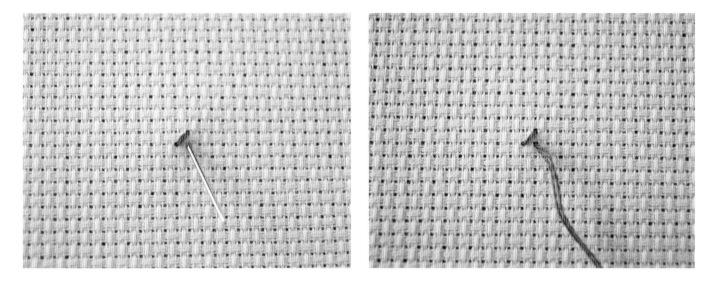

7. Complete your cross by pushing your needle through the top right corner of your cross, this completes your first stitch with a new thread.

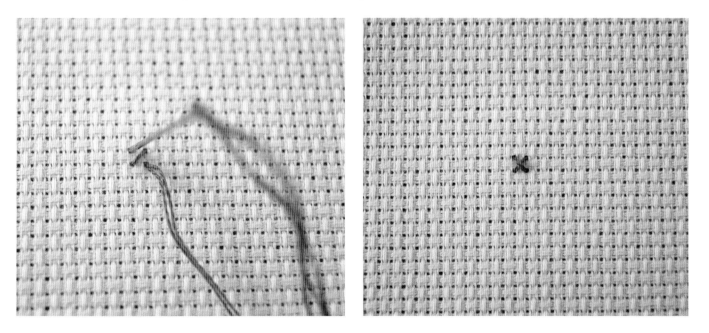

HOW TO CROSS STITCH

Each cross on your fabric is made up of two stitches. The first should go from the bottom left to top right, with the second stitch running from bottom right to top left. In turn, this creates a cross.

 TIP You can vary this as you see fit; however, it will usually look best on your completed piece if all of your second stitches (the one that lays on the top) run in the same direction.

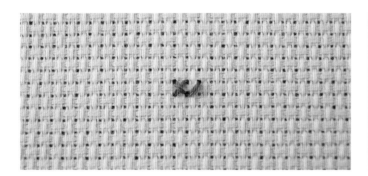 

FINISHING A THREAD

When you have almost finished a piece of thread or need to change colour, on the reverse side of your fabric run your needle behind a few of your stitches.

There is no need to tie a knot, simply finish by trimming down the tail of your thread, this will keep the back of your fabric neat as you continue to stitch.

You can see from the back of this example where I have tied off threads and trimmed the tails to keep them out of the way.

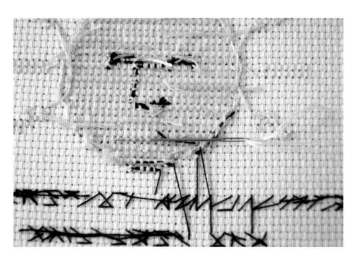 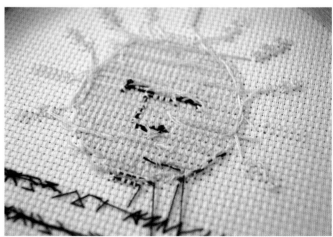

HOW TO BACKSTITCH

Some cross-stitch patterns also include an element of backstitch. If you can see lines on your chart (aside from the grid) these lines will represent backstitches, which are usually stitched with one strand of thread.

For this, you will need to loop the tail of your thread under some stitches on the back of your fabric – because the loop method won't work if you only need to stitch with one strand.

Stitch along the lines shown on your chart, this usually adds detail or text (or both).

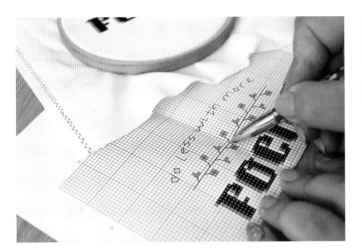 

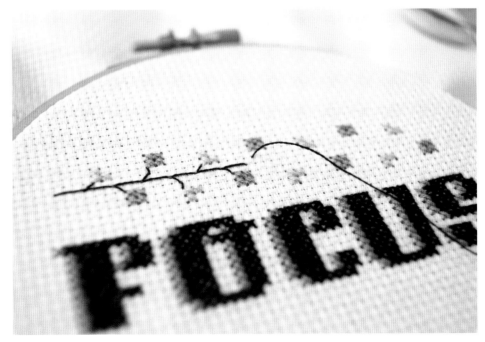

CHAPTER TWO

PRACTISING MINDFUL CROSS STITCH

The act of mindfulness is about focusing solely on the current moment, so in a similar way, practicing mindful stitching is to focus solely on your cross stitch. It involves commitment to be completely in the moment with minimal distractions if you can.

It can be difficult to completely focus your brain, so for any thoughts that side-track your focus it is important not to immediately dismiss them. Instead, acknowledge them and imagine picking them up and removing them from your mind. Then consciously guide your focus back to your stitching.

Another part of being mindful is to be non-judgmental to ourselves and to those around us. If you struggle to focus your brain to begin with, that's ok. Try to go through the process of removing those thoughts and returning your focus to your stitching.

Four Steps to Mindful Cross Stitch

1. Plan Ahead. If you can, schedule in your crafting session and make sure you allow yourself the time needed to relax.

2. Prepare Your Space. Before starting, make sure you have everything to hand that you'll need to get going with your craft. (Craft supplies, snacks, blankets etc.)

3. Remove Distractions. Make sure to turn off or remove any unnecessary distractions from your space. (TV, mobile phone, etc.)

4. Focus and Enjoy. Consciously focus on your stitching and how it makes you feel. Try to relax into the repetitive motion and, most importantly, enjoy.

What people say

I asked a group of lovely volunteers to practise some mindful stitching of their own. Here is what they had to say:

Naomi said, 'I felt proud because I had relaxed and thoroughly enjoyed my time stitching. I really switched off and enjoyed the comforting motion of the stitching.'

Alison noticed that she felt different after stitching too, she said, 'I felt even more connected to the piece. I like the way the thread feels and the sound when it comes through the fabric. It was interesting to take time to notice these things as I don't think I always do. It felt even more calming.'

I feel that Imogen nicely summed up the exercise with: 'It doesn't matter if your mind wonders, the important thing is just about bringing it back.'

On that note, it's time to delve into our first set of projects. Happy stitching x

CHAPTER THREE

MINI MINDFUL STITCHES

When I find my mood deteriorating, sometimes what I need is a short, quick project to give me a little mental boost. I don't always want a project that will take me too long to complete, especially if there is a chance it could become overwhelming.

Within this section, I have specifically designed patterns that are smaller, ideal for beginners and easier to digest as you delve into the mindful elements of cross stitch. Use these projects to start practising the method of Mindful Cross Stitch and focus solely on your stitching. How does the fabric/hoop feel in your hand? What sound does the thread make as you pull it through the holes? Think about each of your senses and how the physical process of cross stitching makes you feel.

Being able to easily pick up and put down a cross-stitch project is one of the things that attracts me to it so regularly. If you find your thoughts wandering or your focus stretched, that's OK. Allow yourself to take a break and come back to it later.

SLOW DOWN SNAIL

When you're feeling overwhelmed, let this little snail remind you that it's always OK to slow down. It's a reminder that I often need too.

Beginners

If you're new to stitching use this pattern as a practice run. It can be your first go to get yourself used to the cross-stitching process and practise as you go along. There are only four thread shades, and the pattern is a basic design, so the slow-stitching nature of cross stitch will allow you to take a moment to really slow down and relax into the calm of crafting.

Experienced Cross Stitchers

If you're an experienced stitcher, use this as an introduction to practising mindfulness as you stitch. Focus solely on the project (no TV in the background or podcast to distract you today). What does the hoop feel like in your hand? Does the thread make a noise as you pull it through the fabric? How do the thread shades complement each other? Try to recognise the little things that you would usually pay no attention to and see how this project makes you feel.

Materials

- 7.5cm (3in) embroidery hoop for stitching
- DMC embroidery thread in the following shades:
  - Black, 310
  - White, BLANC
  - Blue Violet, 341
  - Delft Blue, 799
- Size 24 embroidery needle
- 15x15cm (6x6in) piece of 14 count white aida fabric

Strands: For this design use two strands of thread for cross stitch (or one if using the loop method) and one strand for backstitch.

How to Stitch

1. I really enjoyed stitching this tiny snail and worked my way around the pattern by stitching the black (310) first.

2. This acted as an outline so I could fill in the remaining sections one colour at the time. For the main snail body, I used a half stitch to

fill the section (this is the first leg of your cross in only one direction) so I could then go back and finish the stitches, row by row. This is a method I use a lot when stitching a large section of colour and it ensures that all of my top stitches run in the same direction.

3. I then filled in the stitches on the snail shell, starting with the white spots and using the darker blue thread to fill.

4. To finish the design, I added the backstitch, which is done using one strand of embroidery thread and usually adds text or detail. In this project it adds the text and tiny snail smile.

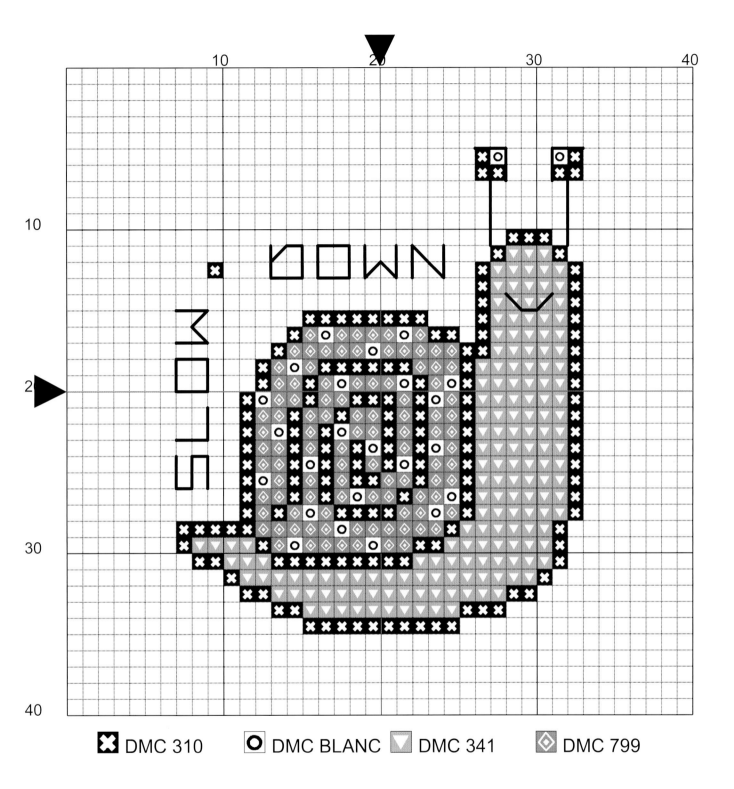

'Apart from food and water, rest is our next most basic and essential need. So why do we feel so bad about giving ourselves time for it?'
The Mindfulness Project, London

What this project means to me

How often do we hear the phrase 'busy as a bee'? Recently, I've been slowing my pace and realising that even the busiest of bees rest sometimes. I feel a lot like this bee, and I too am learning to rest. Often, I'll feel guilty for resting, but it is in these moments that we can really appreciate what beauty is around us.

When I first learnt how to cross stitch I was living in a pretty difficult place. I don't mean physically, we loved our little flat in Sawbridgeworth, but mentally I was struggling to cope with emotions that felt out of control. I found cross stitch to be a welcoming escape from my thoughts and it allowed me to really stop, relax and rest.

Sometimes when life gets busy, or I am feeling low, I notice that I become resistant to resting. My body wants to power through and deal with all of the things that are on my mind, but it is moments like that when I really NEED to rest. I have to force myself to stop and usually that involves some stitching to calm my brain and slow down.

Materials

- 7.5cm (3in) embroidery hoop for stitching
- DMC embroidery thread in the following shades:
  - Black, 310
  - Light Green, 164
  - Light Pink, 604
  - Dark Pink, 602
  - Grey, 647
  - Green, 702
  - Yellow, 743
- Size 24 embroidery needle
- 15x15cm (6x6in) piece of 14 count white aida fabric

Strands: For this design use two strands of thread for cross stitch (or one if using the loop method) and one strand for backstitch.

How to Stitch

1. To stitch this tiny bee, I started with the dark pink thread (602) for the flower outline. This meant that I could start stitching from the centre of my pattern and the centre of my fabric.

2. Once the outline of dark pink was stitched, I moved on to the dark green (702) stalk and light green (164) leaves.

3. I then added the bee to the flower, with DMC shades yellow (743) and black (310).

4. To finish the hoop, I filled in the remaining flower with the paler shade of pink (604).

5. There is no right or wrong way to work through a cross stitch, so please don't feel you have to stitch in the same order as me.

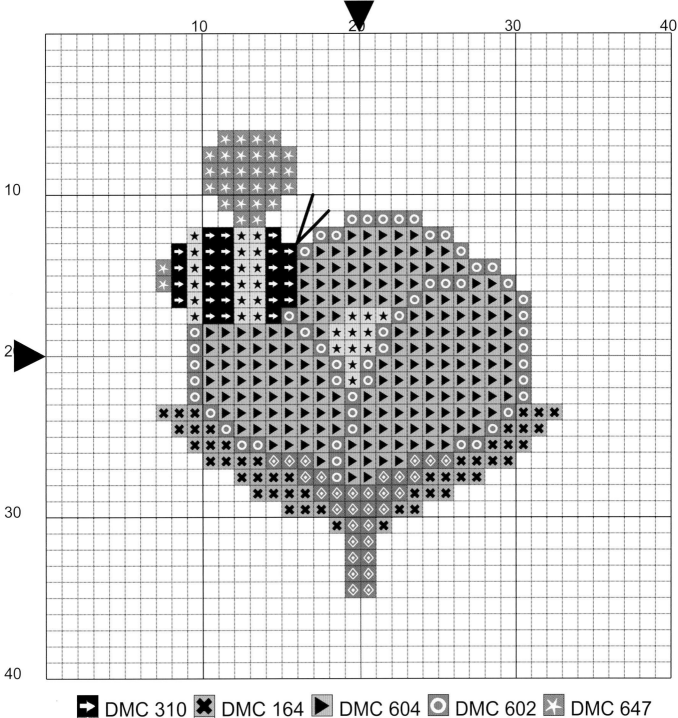

➡ DMC 310 ✖ DMC 164 ▶ DMC 604 ⊙ DMC 602 ✳ DMC 647
◈ DMC 702 ★ DMC 743

The pace of modern-day life can be incredibly quick, and, somehow, we have built up this expectation that everything needs to be done yesterday. We don't have the patience or the time to wait and, actually, we need to recognise that this pace of life isn't always healthy. Sometimes all we need to do is slow down and trust the process.

What this project means to me

Alongside not being very good at resting, I can also be known to jump into things headfirst. Often, I am quick to act and forget to pause and reflect on where I am.

Even from a young age I can remember wanting to catch up with my two older brothers, and for a long time I felt as though I was playing an endless game of catch. My brothers are seven and nine years my senior so when I was finishing high school, they were both in relationships, with marriage and babies soon to be in their future plans. I always felt I was three steps behind and remember longing to grow up and join in.

I met my husband Dan when I was 17 and he really helped me to alter this perspective.

Although we both knew quite early on what we hoped our future would hold, Dan taught me the importance of slowing down and enjoying the journey, rather than looking forward to the next big milestone. Don't get me wrong, I do still love setting goals for the future, but he helps me to appreciate that life is not a race.

Much like the flowers in this hoop, Dan and I have grown together. Slowly discovering who we are as individuals, together as a couple, and more recently as parents too.

This project

This Trust the Process hoop represents how important it is to recognise growth, no matter how small or gradual. In a similar way, the process of cross stitching can also be a slow one. Rather than rush to finish this project, try to focus in on the needle and thread and enjoy the journey, stitch by stitch.

I hope that this hoop will work as a reminder to slow down and enjoy the moment without racing off to the next thing or the next goal; live in the moment mindfully and Trust the Process. Sometimes life can take us on difficult routes, but with determination and self-care we can achieve absolutely anything.

Materials

- 10cm (4in) embroidery hoop for stitching
- DMC embroidery thread in the following shades:
  - Black, 310
  - Brown, 435
  - Violet Light, 554
  - Light Green, 164
  - Yellow, 743
  - Blue, 799
  - White, BLANC
  - Dark Green, 505
  - Violet, 553
- Size 24 embroidery needle
- 18x18cm (7x7in) piece of 14 count white aida fabric

Strands: For this design, use two strands of thread for cross stitch (or one if using the loop method) and one strand for backstitch.

How to Stitch

1. Counting down from the centre of the fabric and pattern, I started stitching with the black (310) to complete the text 'Trust the Process' before moving my way up to the flowerpots.

2. I enjoyed working through the flowerpots one by one, showing the progress of the plants as the project grew.

3. The last piece to stitch was the flowerpot outline in black (310), and the dark green (505) for the plant stalks. Both of these have been stitched with a single strand; however, you may choose to stitch with two strands for a bolder look.

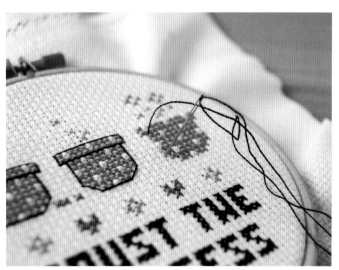

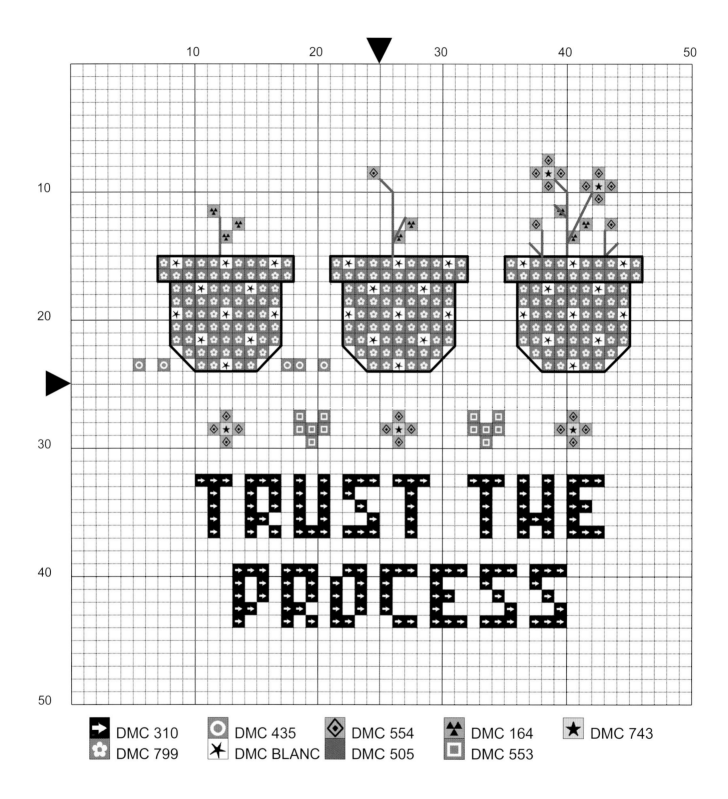

→ DMC 310	◎ DMC 435	◈ DMC 554	⁂ DMC 164	★ DMC 743
✿ DMC 799	✳ DMC BLANC	▨ DMC 505	▣ DMC 553	

TIME FOR POSITIVI-TEA

What this project means to me

It always feels great catching up with a friend over a nice cup of tea. I'm a firm believer that there is little that a cup of tea can't solve.

I've never been the type of person to have a big group of friends; instead I have a few good friends that I know I can always call on. One of my best friends is my mum and if I ever need to talk or cry or share a hug, I'll often go to her, and do you know what we'll do? More often than not, we'll put the kettle on.

I wanted to design a hoop to represent that process of coming together, interacting with family or friends, and sharing what's on your mind. Talking can be invaluable, and when we feel our thoughts are heavy or difficult to talk about, that's when we need it most.

So this is your reminder to phone your pal, arrange to get together and spread some much-needed positivi-tea. You could even arrange a 'crafternoon' and stitch this cute oval hoop together while you catch up.

Materials

- 9x12.5cm (3.5x5in) embroidery hoop for stitching
- DMC embroidery thread in the following shades:
  - Black, 310
  - Yellow, 744
  - White, BLANC
  - Grey, 648
  - Light Purple, 554
  - Purple, 553
- Size 24 embroidery needle
- 15x18cm (6x7in) piece of 14 count white aida fabric

Strands: For this design use two strands of thread for cross stitch (or one if using the loop method) and one strand for backstitch.

How to Stitch

1. For this project, I started by stitching the black (310) for the mug outline before adding the bee and dark purple shadowing.

2. I then worked to fill the lighter shade of purple into the mug in a block of colour.

 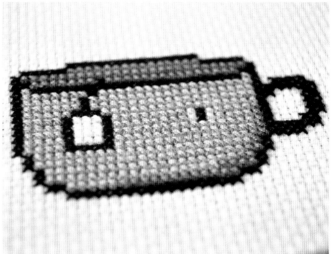

3. To finish, I added the decorative yellow hearts and black backstitch for the text.

Make It Your Own

Try using your own selection of thread shades; you could even match them against your very favourite mug for an extra personal touch.

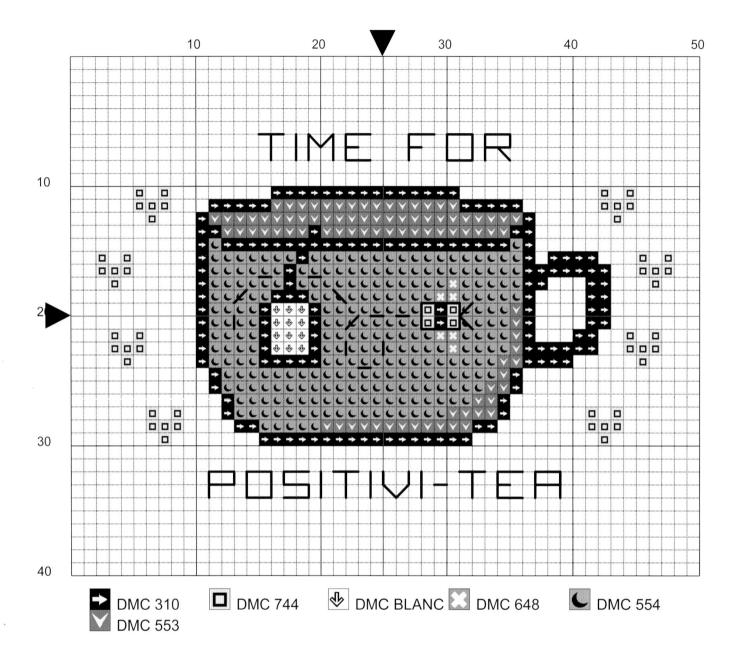

What this project means to me

To me this hoop is a reminder that slowing down can help you reflect and appreciate the smaller things around you.

This design came about after I was asked to work on a community stitching project with seven incredible needlework designers. I was thrilled to be involved and while designing my assigned letter, M, it felt fitting to include the project in my book. I wanted the project to represent me as a cross-stitch designer and where I sit within the community as an artist. To you the letter M might represent a different word, so choose something that feels most poignant to you, it could be that it is a person or a place.

The community collaboration is soon to be revealed and I am very excited to share the 'community over competition' message at the forefront of the project. Special thanks to Amy at Hello Treacle for organising the project and bringing together such a wonderful group of creatives.

Materials

- 10cm (4in) embroidery hoop for stitching
- DMC embroidery thread in the following shades:
  - Black, 310
  - Light Pink, 604
  - Green, 702
  - Light Grey, 648
  - Dark Pink, 602
  - Yellow, 744
  - Light Blue, 341
  - Blue, 799
  - Light Green, 164
  - Purple, 209
  - White, BLANC
- Size 24 embroidery needle
- 18x18cm (7x7in) piece of 14 count white aida fabric

Strands: For this design, use two strands of thread for cross stitch (or one if using the loop method) and one strand for backstitch.

How to Stitch

1. As with a lot of my stitches, I like to begin by working on the outline, so I started with the black (310) before adding the bee to the left and flower to the right.

2. I then stitched the blue (799, one of my favourite shades of blue) as a shadow.

3. Next, I filled the main letter with the light blue shade 341.

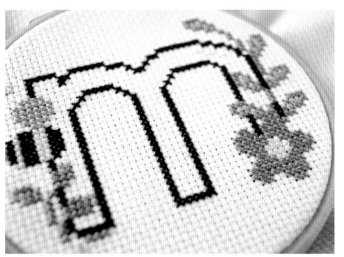

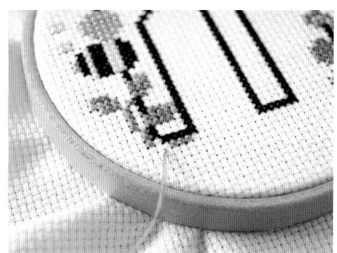

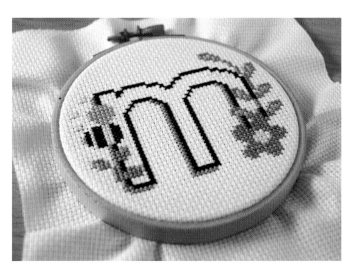

And to finish the hoop, I added the backstitched lettering to complete the message.

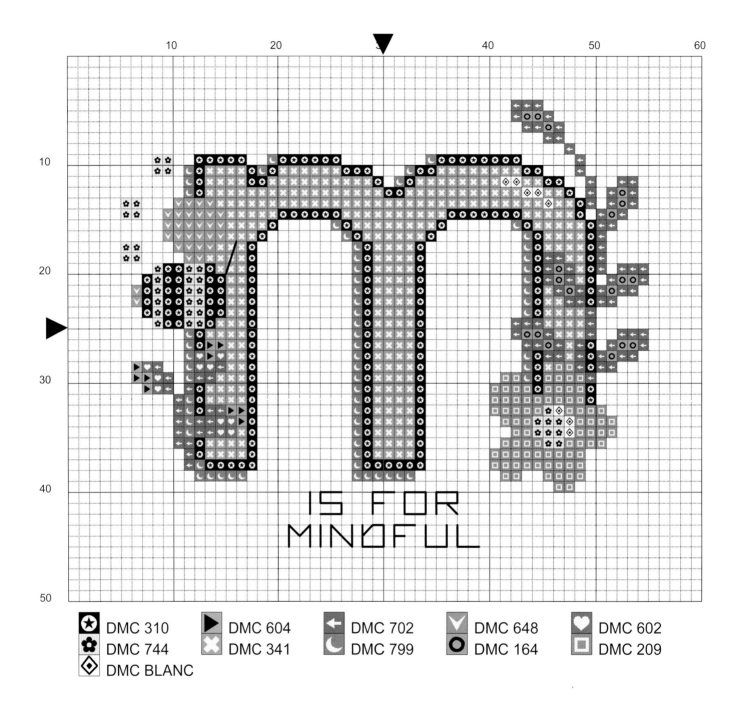

✪ DMC 310	▶ DMC 604	◀ DMC 702	✔ DMC 648	♥ DMC 602
✿ DMC 744	✕ DMC 341	☾ DMC 799	○ DMC 164	▣ DMC 209
◈ DMC BLANC				

CHAPTER FOUR

POSITIVE AFFIRMATIONS

Positive affirmations are short daily reminders that can help you to push the boundaries of your negative thoughts and motivate you forward in your day. These positive phrases can help you remember your value and worth. They also allow you to share calm, happy messages with the special people around you. If you have a friend who is going through a difficult time, stitch them a positive affirmation to focus their attention and bring that extra sense of self-love into their life.

I recently had the pleasure of talking to crafter, Imogen, about her own experiences of crafting for calm. We talked generally about our love for cross stitch and touched upon the importance of positive affirmations and how they can become influential without you even realising. Imogen said 'I tend to gravitate towards cross stitch patterns which have positive affirmations... stitching them helps increase my positive thinking. Even if I don't believe the quote, it gets in my head and then the finished project acts as a reminder. I now have them dotted around my home and I even have one on my desk at work.'

Within this chapter, I have designed five different positive affirmations that I hope will influence how you see yourself, just like Imogen. Each project holds a different uplifting message and I'll share why that quote or phrase feels so powerful to me personally. Over the next few projects, I'll talk about why I always feel determined to prove people wrong and how my childhood helped me to become the person I am today. I will also share with you why my favourite friendship is with someone who I don't talk to much and how it is important to 'stay in your own lane' when things get tough.

I hope each of these projects will resonate with a moment or period in your life and you will stitch each hoop feeling empowered and motivated to prove the doubters wrong.

What this project means to me

I can't even count the number of times I've been told I couldn't do something. Whether it's because I was too young, because I am a woman, or, more recently, because I am a female business owner (it's clear that some people don't like that combination).

An example of this can often be seen in news stories or headlines, when we are reminded how much less likely you are to be successful if you are from a 'broken home'. As someone who falls into this category, I am thankful that these statistics make me laugh. If I weren't so self-assured, could this make me feel destined for failure? Probably.

If nothing else, challenges and emotional setbacks like this have given me a ton of motivation to prove people wrong.

Having the confidence to prove people wrong goes hand in hand with crafting and the improvement it can make not only to our mental well-being but also to our self-esteem. Fellow needlework enthusiast Sara, who runs her own creative business, shares an interesting summary of this very topic: 'It's not only the dopamine inducing effects or meditative qualities that make crafting a great tool for your mental health, but it can also improve self-esteem. Trying and succeeding at a new skill, seeing a project progress to completion, and receiving praise for our creations can all help with confidence and improve how we view ourselves.' Sara Davey, Pixels & Purls

This project

This hoop represents any internal battle against negativity that you might be facing in your life. I wanted the design to be simple and bold, so chose leaves and colourful flowers to decorate this strong message.

I hope you'll find this hoop empowering to stitch and display with pride in your home. It should act as a powerful reminder that you are capable of wonderful things.

Materials

- 10cm (4in) embroidery hoop for stitching
- DMC embroidery thread in the following shades:
  - Black, 310
  - Pink, 3806
  - Yellow, 743
  - Green, 702
  - Blue, 799
  - Dark Green, 505
- Size 24 embroidery needle
- 18x18cm (7x7in) piece of 14 count white aida fabric

Strands: For this design use two strands of thread for cross stitch (or one if using the loop method).

How to Stitch

To start this cross stitch, I began by stitching the black (310) for the text. By starting here, you can easily count out from the text to position your leaves and flowers around the hoop. Once I had stitched the text, I moved on to the leaves in the two shades of green thread.

I finished by stitching the flowers which give the hoop a lovely pop of colour. I stitched each of these with a half cross-stitch and then went back to finish each of the crosses.

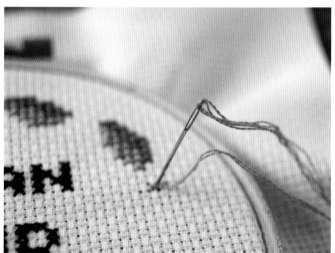

Make It Your Own

Choose your own favourite shades of thread for the flowers and make the hoop unique to you.

➡ DMC 310	☑ DMC 3806	✶ DMC 743	⊙ DMC 702	✕ DMC 799

☐ DMC 505

What this project means to me

Ever since I started working on this project, I knew what I needed to write about to help summarise how this hoop makes me feel - and that is my relationship with my mum. I have already mentioned that my mum is one of my best friends and she taught me to believe in myself, even from a very young age.

My parents separated when I was 5 and although I still have contact with my dad, growing up predominantly in a single-parent home with my two older brothers was challenging at times. I was young and peacefully ignorant to it at the time, but looking back, I realise just how hard my mum worked for us. I don't remember us having holidays abroad or big expensive presents, but we never went without what we needed. My mum worked in multiple jobs and it meant I spent a lot of time with my brothers, pretend-wrestling in the living room and out on our bikes with their friends. The determination and strong personality always shown by my mum, definitely rubbed off on me; there is no doubt that it has helped me to become the person I am today.

My mum has always pushed me to be the best version of me that I can be and I will always be grateful for that. It feels fitting to dedicate this hoop to her – thank you Mum. Just like you, I can do amazing things.

Materials

- 10cm (4in) embroidery hoop for stitching
- DMC embroidery thread in the following shades:
  - Black, 310
  - Green, 164
  - Light Blue, 341
  - Light Yellow, 744
  - Yellow, 743
  - Blue, 799
  - Purple, 553
  - Red, 666
  - Orange, 947
- Size 24 embroidery needle
- 18x18cm (7x7in) piece of 14 count white aida fabric

Strands: For this design use two strands of thread for cross stitch (or one if using the loop method).

How to Stitch

1. Working on this project, I decided to stitch one colour section at a time. I started with the text for 'I can do' and proceeded to stitch in order of the rainbow threads.

2. I loved seeing the rainbow and 'Amazing' text come to life section by section, with the sunshine and cloud being added alongside.

➡ DMC 310	⚑ DMC 164	✖ DMC 341	✿ DMC 744	☽ DMC 743
⊙ DMC 799	▣ DMC 553	▲ DMC 666	↑ DMC 947	

What this project means to me

I'm fairly sure comparison is the root of all evil, but even so, I still find myself stuck in a comparison loop sometimes. Whether it's comparing my business, my house, or the way I parent, there is always something that someone is doing better than me – but that doesn't mean I am any less a businesswoman, wife or mother.

Sometimes when I can feel that comparison creeping up on me, I remind myself to 'stay in my own lane' because it doesn't matter what anyone else is doing, I need to fully focus on me. This hoop represents the feeling that it doesn't matter where I am on my journey, 'I am exactly where I need to be.'

From time to time, I try to consciously take a step back and reflect on where I am and how far I have come. It is so important to look back and appreciate what you have and, although we are guilty of always wanting what someone else has, remember that there is probably someone comparing their life to yours and thinking the very same thing.

I hope that this hoop will be your reminder; that you too, are exactly where you need to be.

Materials

- 13cm (5in) embroidery hoop for stitching
- DMC embroidery thread in the following shades:
  - Black, 310
  - Sky Blue, 519
  - Green, 164
- Size 24 embroidery needle
- 20x20cm (8x8in) piece of 14 count white aida fabric

Strands: For this design, use two strands of thread for cross stitch (or one if using the loop method) and one for backstitch.

How to Stitch

1. For this project I tried to start stitching from as close to the centre of the hoop as possible. I chose to start off with the small swirl of blue thread below the text. From here, I could count my stitches down to each of the butterflies.

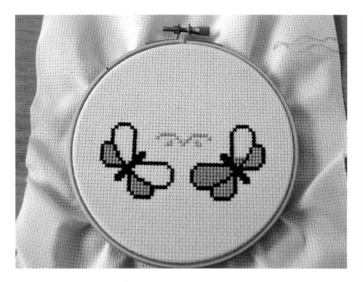 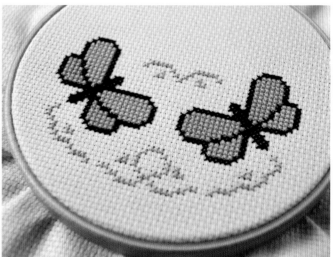

2. To finish the design, I added the swirls which work as a pretty border, adding the backstitched text to the hoop as the final part.

Make It Your Own

I chose a minimal thread palette for this design because I love how these shades of blue and green complement each other. Try using a wider selection of threads to stitch the butterflies and create your own personal hoop.

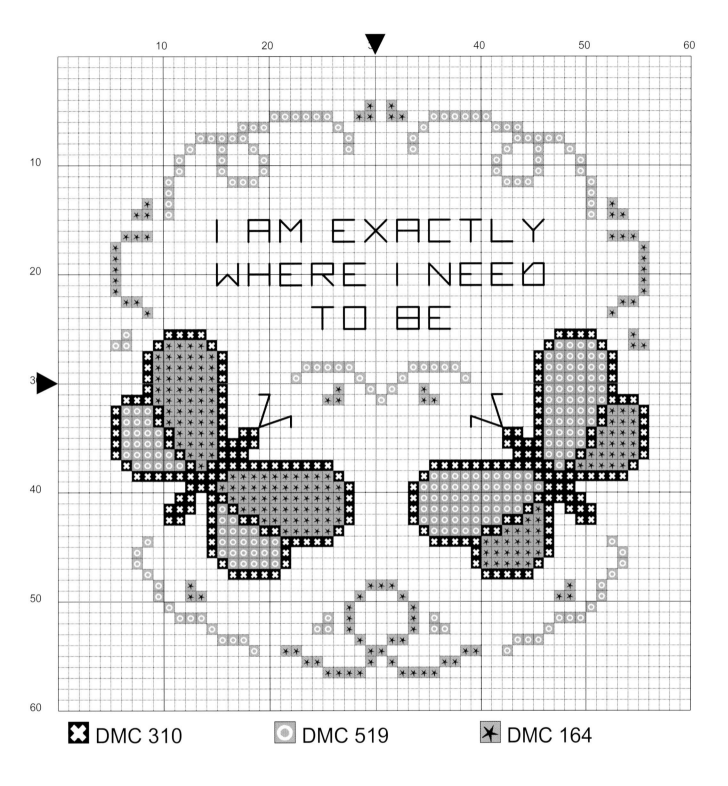

✖ DMC 310 **◉** DMC 519 **✱** DMC 164

What this project means to me

I wanted to fill this book with important phrases and special quotes that I live my life by. This particular hoop acts as a reminder that every single day is a chance for a new beginning, a fresh start and an exciting new opportunity to fill your day with positive interactions. Sometimes you need to take things one day at a time, so I hope this mini hoop will give you that positive reminder each morning.

If every day is a new day, then it is deserving of a fresh start and a clear slate.

When designing this hoop, I opted for simple pastel shades and the use of blank space for the text. I love what it represents, and the message it portrays. What will you do today to give yourself a fresh start?

Materials

- 10cm (4in) embroidery hoop for stitching
- 8cm (3in) embroidery hoop to display your finished stitching
- DMC embroidery thread in the following shades:
  - Green, 164
  - Blue, 341
  - Yellow, 744
- Size 24 embroidery needle
- 18x18cm (7x7in) piece of 14 count white aida fabric

Strands: For this design use two strands of thread for cross stitch (or one if using the loop method).

How to Stitch

1. This design only contains three thread shades; however, they are each quite large chunks of colour. I started my hoop by stitching the blue sky in shade 341. I stitched this gradually, row by row, making sure to leave blank space for the lettering.

2. I then stitched the green (164) for the grass and finished the hoop with a pastel shade (744) for the sunshine.

3. I stitched this project in a 4in embroidery hoop and then transferred the fabric into a 3in hoop to frame. You may wish to do the same; however, this stage is optional and depends on which look you prefer.

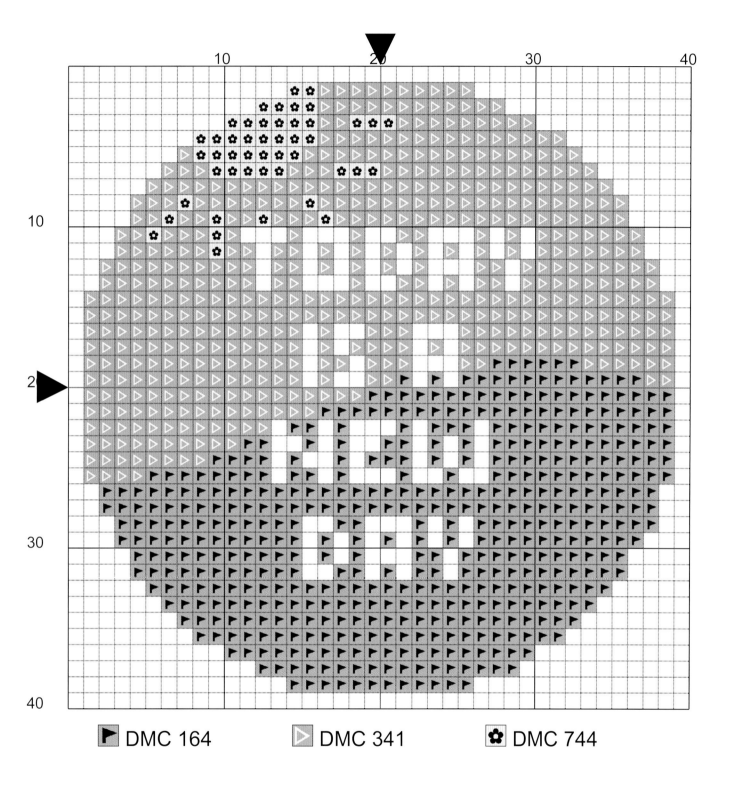

DMC 164   ▷ DMC 341   ✿ DMC 744

What this project means to me

Throughout my adult life, I have learnt to surround myself with people who allow me to be the truest authentic version of me. At times, I have stepped back from relationships that felt toxic or one-sided and leaned into those that make me feel fulfilled and comfortable in my own skin. One friendship that has survived the test of time is with my friend Lorna, and I'm going to tell you why it's so special.

Lorna and I have been friends since school, but what's nice about our friendship is that it has never required a lot of 'maintenance'. I don't feel bad for not messaging her for weeks at a time and equally she won't be offended or mad at me if I forget to respond to a message because something (usually a toddler) distracted me when I read it (it happens a lot, sorry Lorna). But regardless of that, I know I can call on her any time of the day or night and she'll be there, and she knows I would be for her.

We don't speak every day or even every week, but we make time for each other when it matters. When I signed my book deal, she was there at the earliest opportunity, peering through my front door with a bottle of prosecco in hand because she knew how much of a special moment that was for me. We hadn't caught up with each other in a few weeks but that afternoon we chatted and laughed, and it is in moments like that when I remember why we have such a great friendship. I was completely and utterly 'free to be me'.

As you stitch this colourful floral hoop, think about someone in your life who makes you feel completely free to be yourself. Who can you truly let your hair down with?

Materials

- 9x12.5cm (3.5x5in) embroidery hoop for stitching
- DMC embroidery thread in the following shades:
  - Black, 310
  - Dark Pink, 602
  - Pink, 604
  - Pale Pink, 808
  - Yellow, 744
  - Blue, 799
  - Light Blue, 341
  - Dark Purple, 333
  - Purple, 209
- Size 24 embroidery needle
- 15x18cm (6x7in) piece of 14 count white aida fabric

Strands: For this design, use two strands of thread for cross stitch (or one if using the loop method).

How to Stitch

1. With an oval embroidery hoop, take extra care when placing your fabric into the hoop to ensure that the fabric is straight. I started working through this project by stitching the text first, which is in black thread (310).

2. I then worked my way through the other threads, adding colour to the hoop one flower at a time.

➡️ DMC 310 ❤️ DMC 602 ⬜ DMC 604 🚩 DMC 818 ✿ DMC 744
⚪ DMC 799 ▷ DMC 341 ★ DMC 333 ∨ DMC 209

CHAPTER FIVE

GUEST INTERVIEW

THE IMPORTANCE OF MOVING YOUR MINDSET WITH AMY ODD

As we reach a halfway point in the book, I'd like to introduce Amy Odd, of Moving Mindset Hypnotherapy, who I can proudly now refer to as my former therapist. Amy is a clinical hypnotherapist and registered nurse, with a specialist interest in the way the mind and body link. During the research for this book, we discussed ways that we can let ourselves practise self-care in a non-judgmental way. Often, we see self-care referred to, in Amy's own words, as 'candlelit baths twinned with five minutes peace from your busy life,' but we agree that it is much more than that. Here we discuss the concept further and how you can introduce this into your everyday routine.

Amy:

One of the keys to true self-care is to find and make your own inner peace and happiness. At times, many of us find ourselves suffering from mental health issues – such as anxiety, depression, confidence crisis and such like. Sometimes we become so overwhelmed that our metaphorical stress bucket becomes full, exacerbating those issues. We can find it difficult to figure out how to improve, because often we don't know how, and at the most crucial time, the self-care we need for our mental health goes out of the window.

So, when we are suffering with mental illness and in desperate need of self-care, that is exactly when we are less inclined to indulge in the practice that will help to mend our minds? So, how do we make this shift?

Amy:

At the forefront of moving your mindset must be the realisation that you cannot continue this way. Once we have the desire to change, we can start to reignite and make new pathways in the brain, thus refocusing our attention. This is where self-care can be so important – if you do not look after yourself, then who will? Only you can make those changes.

I know first-hand what a huge impact changing your mindset can have. Really wanting to make a change and taking that first step can feel like such a release. But how does changing your mindset have such an impact on your mental wellness? And is there a way we can take action straight away?

Amy:

Think of the act of self-care for your mindset as brain training. We know that in order to be different, we need to think differently and act differently also. Follow the exercise below to get you started with this, considering along the way that you are encouraging your mindset to improve. Be consistent, committed and revisit the task daily – the brain likes repetition in order to improve.

Amy has kindly provided an exercise that will help you to take the first steps in shifting your mindset. Each day, write down at least one thing for each of the categories listed below. There is a printable version available to download, which we have condensed to a one-page weekly worksheet. Visit www.movingmindset.co.uk/mindful-cross-stitch to start your exercise today.

Thoughts
What positive thoughts have you had today and what good has come from them? (You could link these to the affirmations in this book.)

Action
What one thing have you done today that you feel good about or that has helped you to move forwards? (i.e., stitching).

Interactions
Have you spoken to someone today who has made you smile? Perhaps you met up with a good friend? We know that a support network is often good for our mental health.

What has been good about your day today?
Write a few points about the highlights of your day, ensuring that you consider why they have been good.

REMEMBER – Look after your mind, and the rest will fall into place.

CHAPTER SIX

SELF-CARE STITCHES

This chapter explores the importance of indulgently leaning into self-care. It is vitally important to look after ourselves, especially when the stresses of everyday life start to become overwhelming.

At the beginning of 2022, I realised I was struggling to keep on top of my emotions. I felt as though my mind was out of control and realised I had slowly reached a state of depression. It is a place that feels quite alien to me now, but during that time I went through a very dark cloud of emotion.

The three years prior had been spent growing a successful business, bringing up a happy, life-of-the-party toddler and trying to be a pretty decent wife at the same time. On one hand I was focusing on all of the really good things in my life but on the other I had completely lost touch with my own self-care, and for a short while I lost 'Sophie'.

Starting therapy sessions with Amy Odd felt like the first major step in my wellness journey. Over time, Amy helped me to recognise and process my feelings, and gradually, I started seeing the authentic, confident 'Sophie' return to my life.

During this self-care themed chapter, I will share more about my journey with Amy and how spreading sunshine and positivity can not only bring joy to your life but to so many others as well.

What this project means to me

I have been digging into my own feelings a lot over the last few months and one of the things I have learnt is that I need to allow myself more time to rest and indulge in self-care.

Self-care can come in many forms and will look different for many people. Your self-care practices might be making sure you get enough sleep, going for regular walks in nature, doing some yoga… or it might be taking time out and indulging in something fun that is just for you - cross stitch for example.

I've always been guilty of running my life at 100mph. Someone asked me a few days ago 'do you ever stop?' and it made me sit back and reflect. No, I don't. Over recent years especially, juggling self-employed life with a toddler has been busy. I wouldn't change a thing, but I do recognise that I'm not very good at stopping. I don't let myself pause and I often feel guilty for taking a break. My brain is always thinking of the next thing, what to do next or what I should be doing now and sometimes the answer is simply, nothing.

During my therapy with Amy (see chapter overview) she gave me a recording to listen to each night before bed. There is one quote that always feels powerful, and I often find myself mouthing the words along with the tape to make them really sink in. It says, 'You don't have to be anywhere; you don't have to do anything,' and this is often the reminder I need to just let go.

This hoop is permission, if you needed it, to allow yourself to indulge in self-care and, more importantly, to never feel guilty about it.

Materials

- 10cm (4in) embroidery hoop for stitching
- DMC embroidery thread in the following shades:
  - Black, 310
  - Green, 702
  - Light Green, 164
  - Light Purple, 554
  - Purple, 553
- Size 24 embroidery needle
- 18x18cm (7x7in) piece of 14 count white aida fabric

Strands: For this design, use two strands of thread for cross stitch (or one if using the loop method) and one for backstitch.

How to Stitch

1. I started this hoop by stitching the black outline of the heart and then moving outwards to the green (702) foliage.

2. The lighter shade of green (164) was added in afterwards and I then worked to fill in the light purple to the centre of the heart.

3. I then moved on to the tiny hearts in purple thread (553).

4. To add the lettering, I used one strand of black (310). Using one strand on my needle, I secured the tail of the thread under some of the stitches on the reverse side of the aida. This anchors the thread and allows me to stitch along the guidelines on the pattern to add in the text: 'Self-Care Isn't Selfish'.

 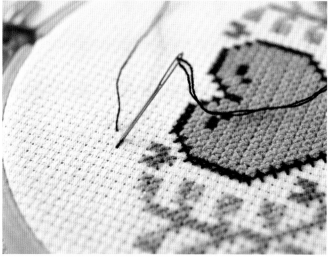

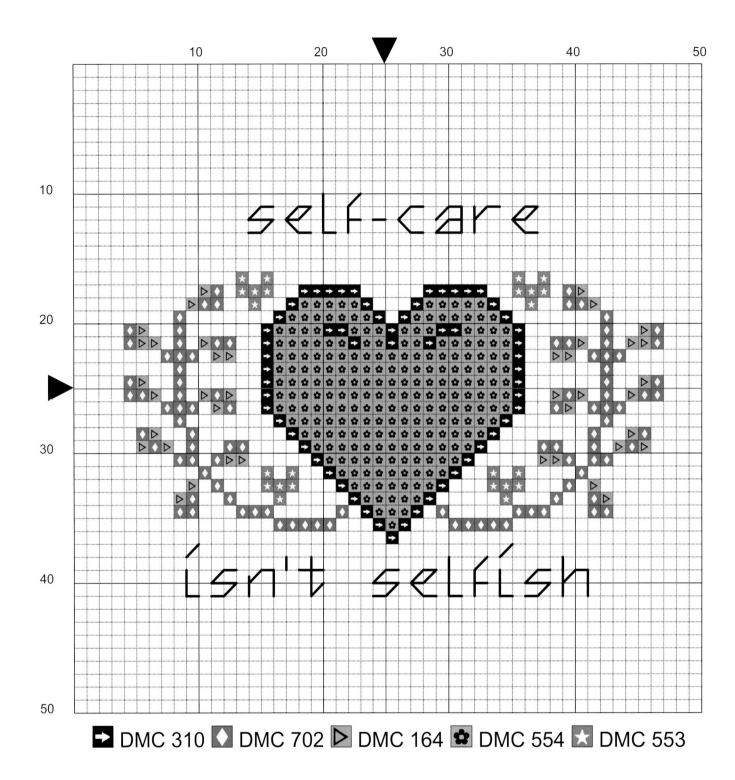

➡️ DMC 310 ◆ DMC 702 ▷ DMC 164 ✿ DMC 554 ★ DMC 553

LET YOURSELF BLOOM

'When we take the time to work on ourselves, it increases our resilience and inner strength.' The Mindfulness Project, London

What this project means to me

When I started therapy, I knew I was setting out on a journey, but I didn't really know where it would take me. During my sessions, Amy and I spoke a lot about who Sophie was and where the old Sophie had been left behind. I am not ashamed to say that those sessions were difficult. I didn't know the answers to a lot of the questions I was being asked, but it gave me a lot to think about. One day something seemed to click, and I realised I wasn't on a journey to find the old Sophie, I was slowly rediscovering a new Sophie. I was listening to my body and understanding my emotions. Without realising it, I was blooming into a new, confident and very true version of myself.

I wanted this hoop to represent the journey I have been on and the process of mental growth. I have recognised the parts of me I was subconsciously holding back, and I now feel more comfortable to let those parts of my personality bloom.

Materials

- 15cm (6in) embroidery hoop for stitching
- DMC embroidery thread in the following shades:
  - Black, 310
  - Green, 702
  - Dark Pink, 602
  - Pink, 604
  - Yellow, 743
  - Purple, 553
  - Light Purple, 554
  - White, BLANC
  - Blue, 799
  - Light Blue, 341
  - Brown, 436
- Size 24 embroidery/tapestry needle
- 23x23cm (9in) piece of 14 count white aida fabric

Strands: For this design, use two strands of thread for cross stitch (or one if using the loop method) and one for backstitch.

How to Stitch

1. To start this project, I stitched the shelf in tan brown (436) to give me a good central point to work from.

2. I then decided to stitch the text, which calls for black (310).

3. Next, I made my way up to the flowers. I really enjoyed the process of seeing the flowers slowly come together and take shape in their brightly coloured vases.

Make It Your Own

I chose a bright and vibrant colour palette for the flowers, but you may prefer working with a more pastel-based thread selection. Play around with your favourite thread shades and see what you create.

➡ DMC 310	▷ DMC 702	♥ DMC 602	⊙ DMC 604	◈ DMC 743
◣ DMC 553	⇩ DMC 554	★ DMC BLANC	▼ DMC 799	☽ DMC 341
◳ DMC 436				

LOVE YOURSELF FIRST

What this project means to me

Do you love yourself unconditionally? I'm not sure I could answer yes to this question, but I am working hard to get there.

For a long time, I have struggled to be completely confident in my own skin and have yo-yo dieted for most of my adult life. My husband Dan and I have been together for over thirteen years and in that time, I have been a size 12, a size 20 and everything in between. The only time I ever relaxed into my body and truly loved myself was during pregnancy. After years of mentally beating myself up for not having a perfect waist, I was blessed with a baby bump and the desire to be slim temporarily dissipated.

After Henry was born, I remember feeling like superwoman and in complete awe of my body, but before long those insecurities returned, and I was swept back into dislike for my body.

Part of self-care is loving yourself and taking time to look after your body and your mind. Personal insecurities like this can often get in the way of that and we end up spending too much of our energy focusing on the negatives.

This project represents the need to Love Yourself First, before anything else.

Materials

- 15cm (6in) embroidery hoop for stitching
- DMC embroidery thread in the following shades:
  - Black, 310
  - Light Pink, 604
  - Tan Brown, 436*
  - Dark Pink, 602
  - Green, 702
  - Light Green, 164
- Size 24 embroidery needle
- 23x23cm (9in) piece of 14 count white aida fabric

*Use your preferred thread shade to represent your own skin tone. Alternatively, use bright vibrant shades of pinks, purples, or blues to fill in the hands for a more creative and abstract hoop.

Strands: For this design use two strands of thread for cross stitch (or one if using the loop method).

How to Stitch

1. I started stitching this project by completing all of the black (310) stitches first.

2. This gave me an outline for each section and allowed me to go back and fill in each section with the required colour.

3. I then chose to add some green foliage around the hands, representing nourishment and growth; however, you can treat this as an optional add-on.

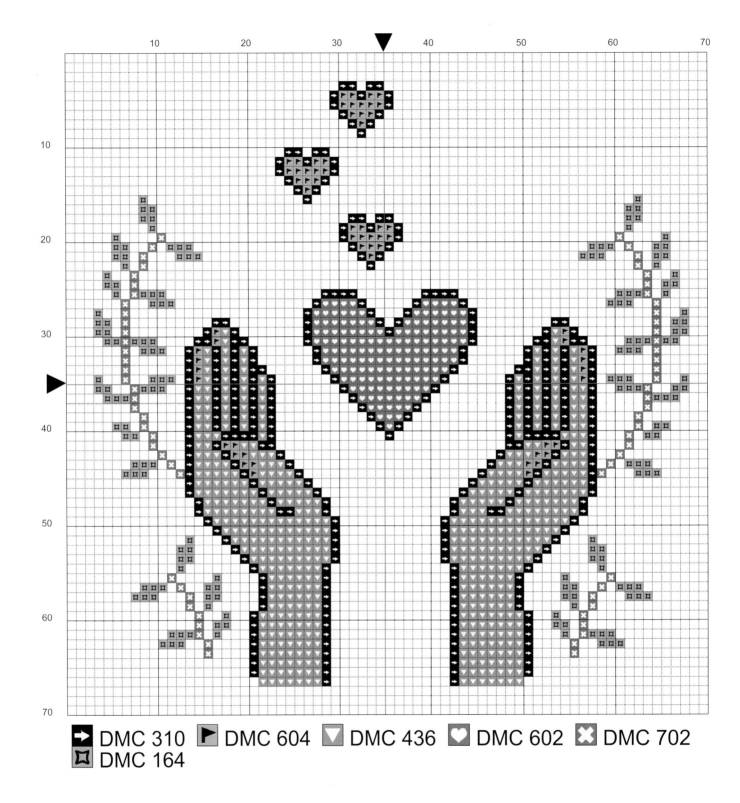

➡️ DMC 310 🚩 DMC 604 🔽 DMC 436 🤍 DMC 602 ❌ DMC 702

🔲 DMC 164

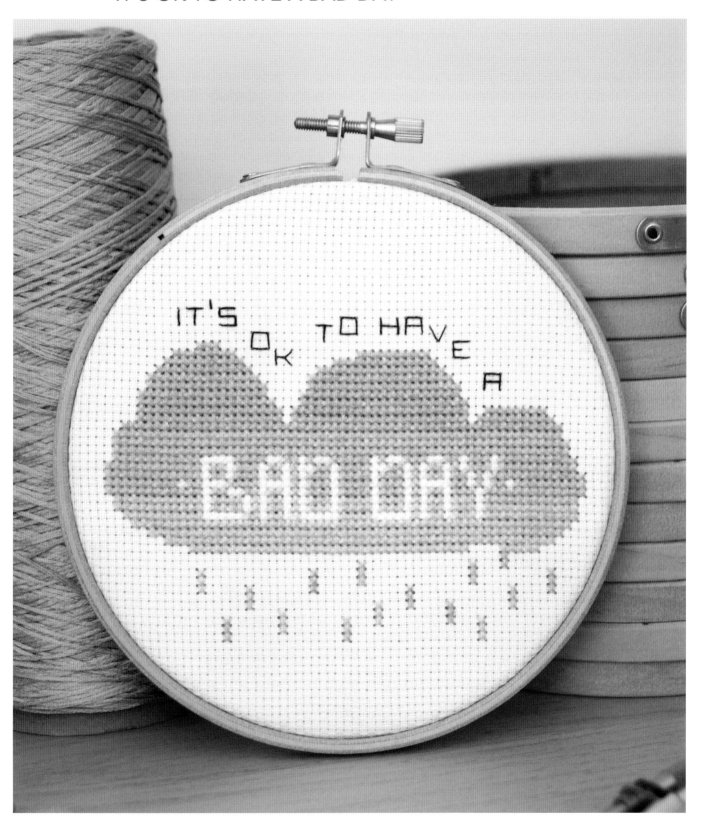

What this project means to me

Therapy has taught me a lot of things, among them is the ability to look for the positives in every day and to embrace that not everything can be perfect all of the time.

Bad days will come, although even in dark moments there are positives to be found, seeking them out can be tricky. But they are there when you start to intentionally look for them. In a similar way, bad days can also bring new opportunities and different perspectives.

As someone who has always been a bit of a perfectionist, making mistakes is not something I find easy to admit to. Admission of error comes alongside feelings of inadequacy and, in the past, the two have led me down a path of negative thoughts.

While working on my mindset and recovering to a place of stability and general wellness, I can recognise now that mistakes are often just a part of the process. You learn a great deal more when you make an error and overcoming those challenges can help you to grow into a more resilient human.

Fellow author, creative and needlework artist, Clare Albans, talks about this in the introduction to her book, *Colourful Fun Embroidery*. She shares the reality that I'm sure many of us will recognise, in that if something we've spent time creating 'doesn't look as perfect as someone else's… we give up on it'.

But this barrier 'can be overcome' she goes on to say, explaining that 'If I'm in a place where I'm open to making mistakes, then I actually find that I am more creative. Learning from your mistakes as part of the creative process is an important lesson, because that's how we learn a craft and how we develop it.' Clare Albans, Hello! Hooray!

Much like Clare, I have learnt to accept mistakes in my work. Often within the cross-stitch community, stitchers are proud to share the 'uniqueness' in their project, which could also be construed as mistakes. Learning to embrace them and reinterpret them as a positive is a really important step.

It's OK to have a bad day, but use that time to rest, reset and reflect on how you'll make sure that tomorrow is a good day.

Materials

- 13cm (5in) embroidery hoop for stitching
- DMC embroidery thread in the following shades:
  - Black, 310
  - Blue Violet, 341
  - Green, 164
  - White, BLANC
  - Sky Blue, 519
- Size 24 embroidery needle
- 20x20cm (8in) piece of 14 count white aida fabric

Strands: For this design, use two strands of thread for cross stitch (or one if using the loop method) and one for backstitch.

How to Stitch

1. To begin this project, I started by locating the centre of my fabric and the centre of my pattern. Using white thread (BLANC), I stitched the text 'Bad Day' first to give me something to stitch the cloud around. I would not normally recommend starting a project with white thread on to white fabric, but there are only a few stitches, and it makes the rest of the project much easier to work through. I then worked through one colour at a time to stitch the cloud.

2. Doing blocks of colour in a half stitch first means that you can count your stitches quickly on to your fabric. You can then return to each row of stitches and complete them without having to particularly follow the pattern. This is a great way to practise mindfulness as the stitching will require less concentration.

3. Once I had stitched the cloud, I worked my way through the raindrops and then moved on to add the backstitched text.

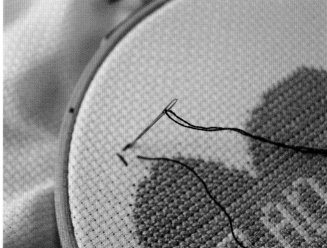

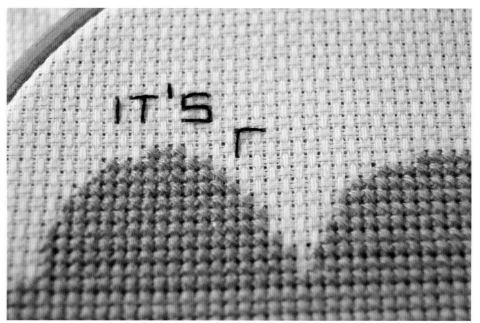

Play around with alternative thread shades to create your very own bad day cloud. Try adding bright, vibrant rainbow shades or pastel tones and see how it changes the mood of the overall project.

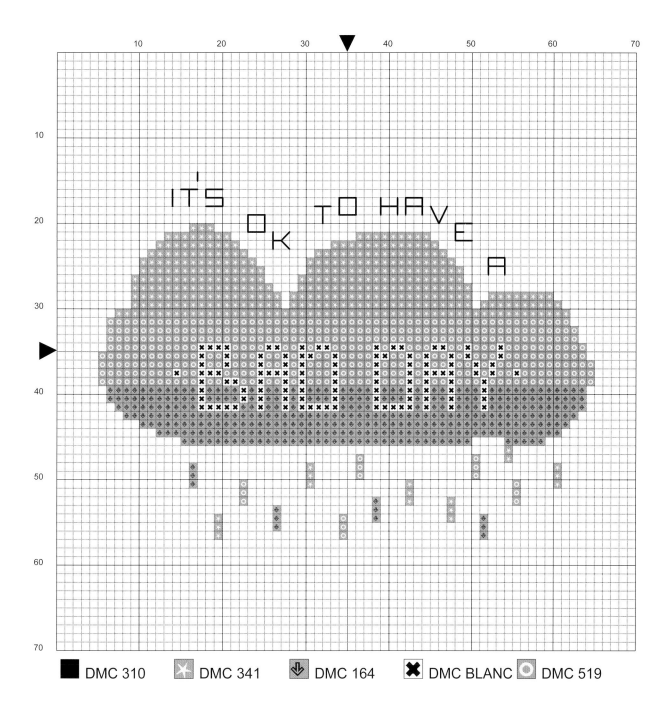

What this project means to me

For me, this hoop represents the need to lean towards the people in your life who feel like sunshine.

Since 2019, the brightest light in my life has been my son. We are often told what a happy, carefree little boy he is and it is so true. From the moment he wakes up in the morning (shouting 'MORNING' at the top of his voice) to the moment he admits defeat to tired eyes at the end of the day, he is the happiest, bounciest little chap. His smile can light up an entire room and he is most certainly my biggest ray of sunshine. This hoop is dedicated to you, Henry. Never stop being our ray of sunshine. I hope you will never stop believing in yourself and continue to be wholeheartedly and unconditionally you.

Materials

- 15cm (6in) embroidery hoop for stitching
- DMC embroidery thread in the following shades:
  - Black, 310
  - Yellow, 743
  - Light Yellow, 744
  - Dark Yellow, 742
  - White, BLANC
- Size 24 embroidery needle
- 23x23cm (9in) piece of 14 count white aida fabric

Strands: For this design, use two strands of thread for cross stitch (or one if using the loop method) and one for backstitch.

How to stitch

1. For this project, I started stitching by adding the black mouth and eyes for the sunshine. From here I could count the stitches out to complete the sunshine, colour by colour.

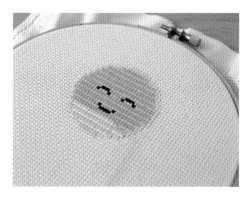 

2. I added the text in a single strand of black (310). Then to finish the hoop, I added the word 'Sunshine' across the bottom along with the rays of sunshine.

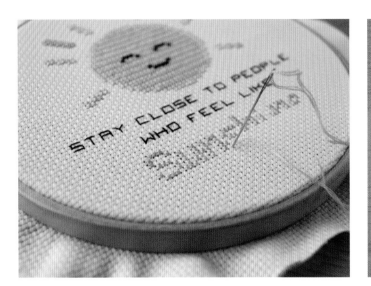

STAY CLOSE TO PEOPLE
WHO FEEL LIKE
SUNSHINE

➡ DMC 310   ◈ DMC 743   ♥ DMC 742   ✱ DMC 744

LOTUS FLOWER

While working through the final cross-stitch project in this chapter, I used the slow nature of stitching to reflect on and appreciate the good things around me. The lotus flower symbolises purity, enlightenment and rebirth and it feels fitting to end this self-care chapter looking forward to the future.

I intentionally left this pattern text-free to allow you to add your own personal meaning to the hoop as you stitch it. What does the lotus flower represent to you?

The splashes of yellow symbolise happiness and warmth with the main palette of purple shades often associated with creativity and ambition. Colour can be so important to a project, so make sure to choose shades that really spark your excitement and creativity.

I love the simplicity of this project because it allows you to really focus on the stitching and lose yourself in the moment. Someone who shares a similar love of mindful crafting is small-business owner and good friend, Bethan Aspland. Bethan often talks about the mindful and calming benefits of sinking into a good creative session. 'As you slow down and pay attention to the colours and patterns involved, you can almost feel your body and mind relaxing and the stresses of life slip away.' Bethan Aspland, Pretty In Paper By B. In a similar way to our mindful stitching technique, try focusing your attention on the colours and textures of your thread and what they mean to you.

Materials

- 13cm (5in) embroidery hoop for stitching
- DMC embroidery thread in the following shades:
  - Light Purple, 211
  - Medium Purple, 210
  - Purple, 209
  - Green, 702
  - Yellow, 743
  - Black, 310
- Size 24 embroidery needle
- 20x20cm (8in) piece of 14 count white aida fabric

Strands: For this design use two strands of thread for cross stitch (or one if using the loop method).

How to Stitch

1. I started stitching this project using the green thread (702) for the flower stem. From here, I stitched the black outline of the main lotus flower shape.

2. This shape allowed me to fill in the different shades of purple into the flower; I worked through them one at a time.

3. To finish the hoop, I added the splashes of yellow.

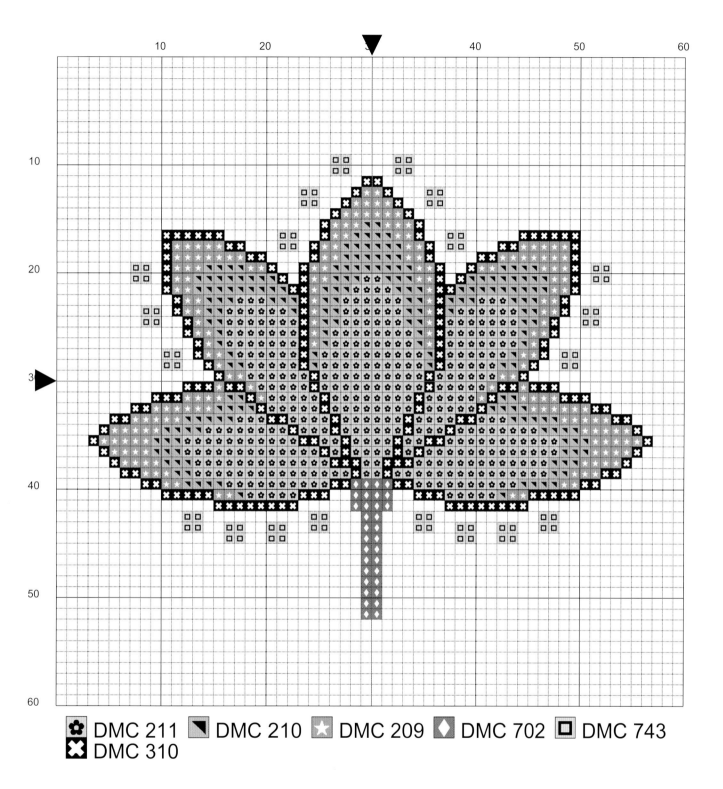

✿ DMC 211   ◥ DMC 210   ★ DMC 209   ◆ DMC 702   ☐ DMC 743
✖ DMC 310

CHAPTER SEVEN

MINDFUL MESSAGES

Within this chapter there are six projects that contain positive mindful messages for you to stitch. In a similar way to positive affirmations, these messages have been selected to bring positivity and mindful awareness into your life.

As we delve more into the mindful elements of stitching, the charity Mind at mind.org.uk has some excellent resources for mindfulness, including the theories behind mindfulness and how it can make a difference to your life:

By using various techniques to bring your attention to the present, you can:

- Notice how thoughts come and go in your mind. You may learn that they don't have to define who you are, or your experience of the world, and that you can let go of them.
- Notice what your body is telling you. For example, you might feel tension or anxiety in your body, such as a fast heartbeat, tense muscles or shallow breathing.

• Create space between you and your thoughts. With this space, you can reflect on the situation and react more calmly.

© Mind. This information is published in full at mind.org.uk

The action of practising mindfulness can take time and may feel unnatural to begin with. Similar to cross stitch, it will feel easier the more you practise. I have found that by practising them together it helps to calm my mind and relieve those everyday stresses.

Throughout these following projects, I'll talk about how looking at things with a new perspective can really make all the difference; why busy life can lead to overthinking; and what small steps we can take to giving ourselves more focus on the things that really matter.

What this project means to me

This colourful stitching theme hoop was not only a joy to design but also to stitch. What I love most about this hoop is the colourful winding threads and the alternative meanings reflected in the quote: 'Unwind and Relax'.

To me, this represents not only the ability to unwind emotionally, but also the physical nature of unwinding your threads and relaxing into the calm nature of stitching.

When I learnt to cross stitch, having the ability to unwind and relax into a project helped me to channel my thoughts more clearly. By taking a break from my busy mind it allowed me to rest and recharge, which is something that doesn't always come easily.

I chatted with Tina, of Titch Stitch UK, about the act of mindful stitching, and she said something that really resonated with me: 'cross stitch is my recharge cycle', and I completely agree with her. She went on to say, 'A good stitching session helps me to regroup and gives me the energy to look at things from a different perspective.'

Of all the projects in this book this is definitely one of my favourites. Although simple in design, the message is an important one and very much represents my own relationship with cross stitch.

Materials

- 15cm (6in) embroidery hoop for stitching
- DMC embroidery thread in the following shades:
    ◦ Black, 310
    ◦ Blue, 799
    ◦ Yellow, 743
    ◦ Pink, 604
    ◦ Purple, 554
    ◦ Green, 164
    ◦ Light Blue, 341
    ◦ Grey, 648
    ◦ Brown, 435
    ◦ Gold, 783
- Size 24 embroidery needle
- 23x23cm (9in) piece of 14 count white aida fabric

Strands: For this design, use two strands of thread for cross stitch (or one if using the loop method) and two for backstitch

How to Stitch

1. To begin stitching this pattern, I worked from the centre of the pattern and fabric to stitch the text, in black (310).

2. From here, I could easily count out on the pattern to stitch the other elements of the design. Next, I chose to stitch the thread skein and twirl of thread at the top, before moving round the hoop on to the needle and thread motifs to decorate.

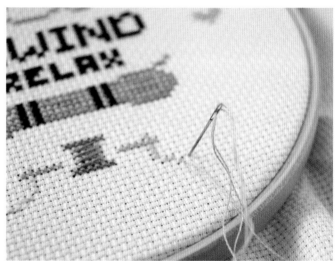

3. For the thread bobbins at the top and bottom of the pattern I used two strands of thread to stitch the diagonal lines, which gives the hoop an added element of texture.

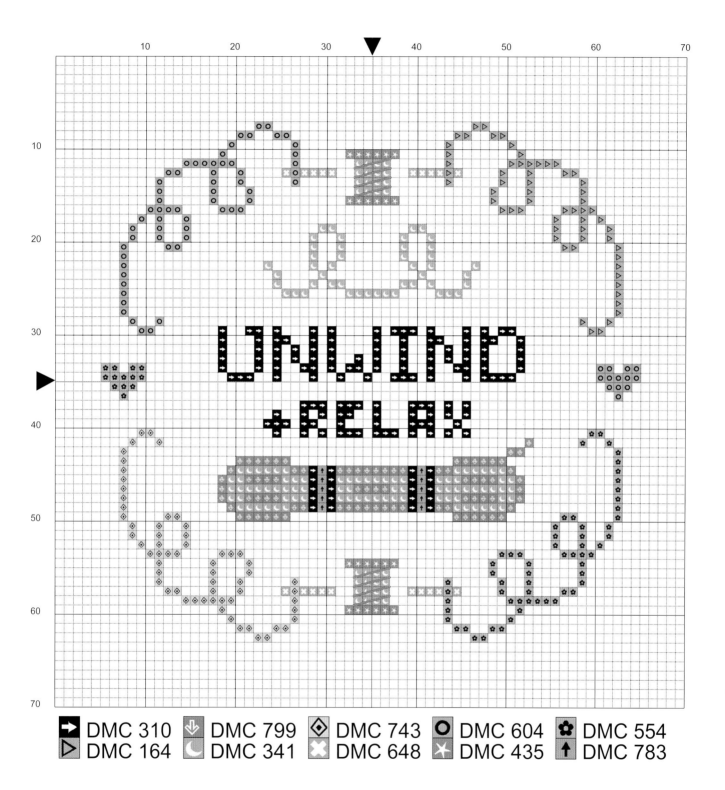

➡ DMC 310   ⬇ DMC 799   ◈ DMC 743   ⊙ DMC 604   ✿ DMC 554

▷ DMC 164   ☾ DMC 341   ✕ DMC 648   ✴ DMC 435   ↑ DMC 783

What this project means to me

I've always been a big goal-setter. I think it comes down to having quite a competitive personality; I have always loved working to a target or setting myself a deadline.

When I first started my business, Sew Sophie Crafts, in October 2019, my goal was to run a successful business and be able to work full time for myself. It was a dream that felt so far-fetched, but I knew it was something I wholeheartedly wanted to achieve - not only for myself but also for my family.

Just one year after setting up my business I was approached and offered a full-time job. The terms were attractive, but I decided to turn it down. It felt bold and brave to say no, but I knew what I wanted to do and that was to nurture and grow my own business. Sew Sophie Crafts was still in its infancy and I didn't want my focus to be pulled away.

The action of turning down that job gave me a huge dose of motivation to prove to myself that I'd made the right decision and to also prove to others that this wasn't a hobby, this would be a success.

That far-fetched dream to be my own boss has been nurtured, loved and cared for and is now my reality. I love the freedom and flexibility it gives me, not only with business decisions but with family life as well.

That goal truly felt like a pipe dream back in 2019 and there have been plenty of bumps along the road, but sometimes I really have to sit and appreciate how far I've come. I am incredibly proud of myself and grateful to every single person who has supported me along the way. It wasn't luck. It grew from hard work, determination, and a whole lot of passion, and if I can do it, so can you.

Dream big. Go for Gold. Don't just set the goal and expect it to arrive at your front door; go forth, nurture that dream and make it happen.

Materials

- 15cm (6in) embroidery hoop for stitching
- DMC embroidery thread in the following shades:
  - Black, 310
  - Dark Green, 505
  - Green, 702
  - Light Green, 164
  - Yellow, 743
  - Pink, 604
  - Purple, 209
  - Sky Blue, 519
- Size 24 embroidery needle
- 23x23cm (9in) piece of 14 count white aida fabric

Strands: For this design, use two strands of thread for cross stitch (or one if using the loop method) and one for backstitch.

How to Stitch

1. To start stitching from the centre of the pattern, I chose to begin by stitching the watering can, starting from the spout.

2. I then added the flowers to the top of the watering can before progressing with the text.

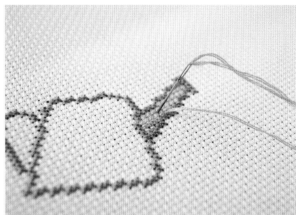

3. To finish the hoop, I added the blue for the sprinkles of water and the remaining flowers.

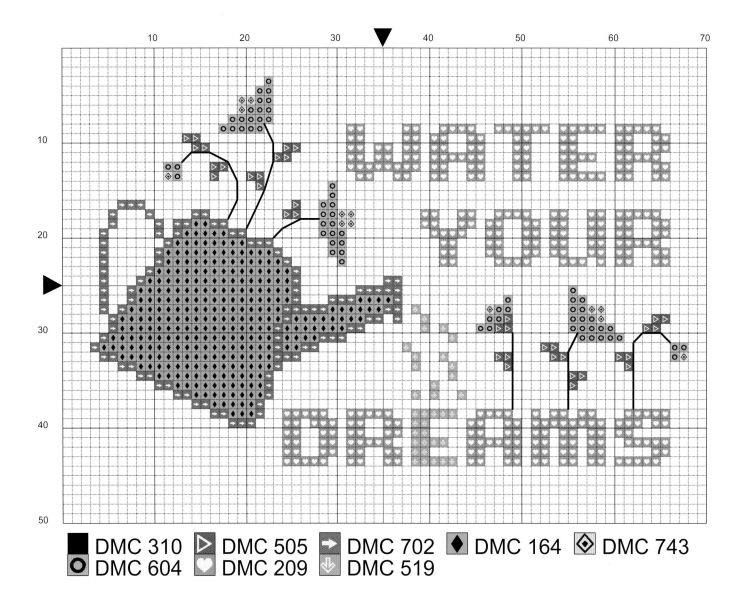

■ DMC 310 ▷ DMC 505 ➡ DMC 702 ◆ DMC 164 ◈ DMC 743
◎ DMC 604 ♥ DMC 209 ⇩ DMC 519

Sometimes things don't go to plan and we hit a bumpy road, but it is important not to allow those disappointments to derail you from your ultimate goal. This quote is a special one and holds a message that I often need reminding of.

What this project means to me

The project is inspired by my good friend Amy, who runs her own creative business, Hello Treacle. Amy and I became friends through the power of the online small-business community, and she happens to be the very same Amy that initiated the community stitching project I mentioned earlier in the book (you'll find this alongside my M is for Mindful hoop, in Mini Mindful Stitches).

You could call us competitors; instead, I am proud to call her my friend. Over time she has become someone I know I can lean on when I hit a bump on my own path and is someone I completely trust. Often my voice of reason and always encouraging me to look at things from a different perspective, this quote always reminds me of her and the overwhelming mantra of community over competition.

Knowing this quote is important to Amy, I asked her if she'd share why these words can feel so powerful. Do you know how she responded? 'These are the words I live by.'

She went on to say, 'Sometimes things don't go to plan and that's OK. Every day we learn something new. When life throws you a curve ball, the trick is to change the plan and not your goal. You'll get there in the end.' Amy Gilbert, Hello Treacle

Know your goal, keep that destination clear in your mind and don't be discouraged when things don't go to plan. How will you change the plan and keep going?

Materials

- 15cm (6in) embroidery hoop for stitching
- DMC embroidery thread in the following shades:
  - Black, 310
  - Red, 666
  - Yellow, 744
  - Blue, 799
  - White, BLANC
  - Grey, 648
  - Pink, 604
- Size 24 embroidery needle
- 23x23cm (9in) piece of 14 count white aida fabric

Strands: For this design, use two strands of thread for cross stitch (or one if using the loop method) and one for backstitch.

How to Stitch

For this pattern I started by stitching the text in the centre of the hoop. I then worked outwards stitching the pattern section by section in a circular motion.

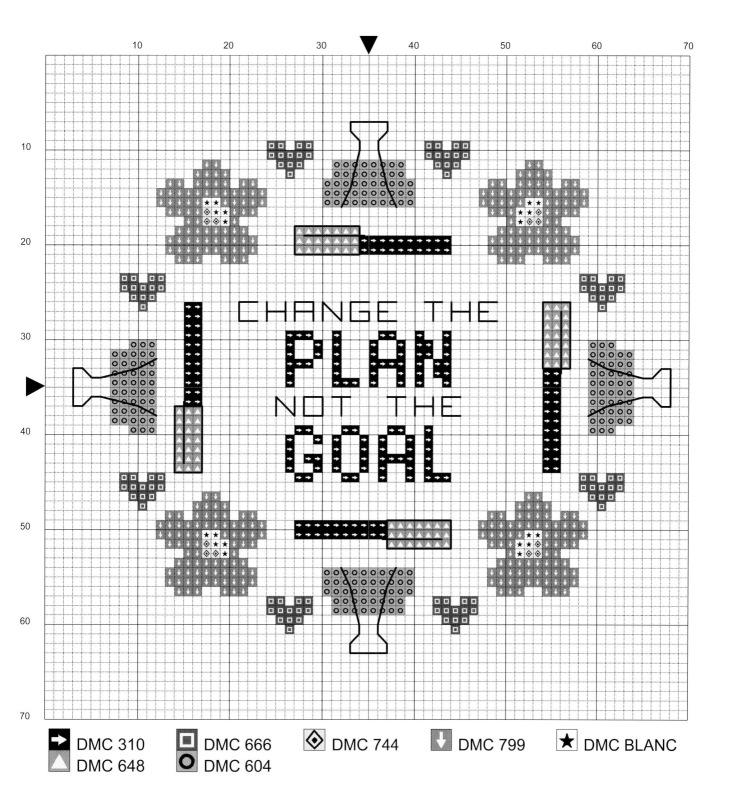

Symbol	DMC	Symbol	DMC	Symbol	DMC	Symbol	DMC	Symbol	DMC
➡	DMC 310	▢	DMC 666	◈	DMC 744	⬇	DMC 799	★	DMC BLANC
▲	DMC 648	⦿	DMC 604						

What this project means to me

I am a chronic overthinker. I will hold my hands up to that. There are certain things I overthink about - usually it's related to being a good enough mum or a successful businesswoman. The worst thing is I am usually aware that I am overthinking, and it still doesn't stop me.

Being a working mum has its challenges, especially when you work from home and don't always have the best balance between work time and family time. Social media is also a guilty pleasure that pulls me away from the things that really matter. When you scroll through the highlights reel from your friends, family, colleagues and sometimes even complete strangers, it is no doubt that we get stuck in that overthinking hole of doom.

Overthinking can often be linked with anxiety. In the lead up to writing this book, many of the people I spoke to expressed similar struggles. Among those conversations were battles with anxiety and depression, along with difficulties coping with some of the general day to day thoughts and feelings they were facing; that was before collectively discovering the mindful benefits of cross stitching.

Mindfulness teaches us to live completely in the moment and this hoop reflects the need to empty (or certainly reduce) those thought bubbles from time to time, not only for our own well-being but so we can focus more on the relationships around us too.

Materials

- 13cm (5in) embroidery hoop for stitching
- DMC embroidery thread in the following shades:
  - Black, 310
  - Tan light, 738*
  - Mahogany, 301*
  - Royal Blue, 797*
  - Blue, 799
  - Light Blue, 341
  - Green, 702
  - Light Green, 164
  - Purple, 553
  - Light Purple, 554
  - Dark Pink, 602
  - Light Pink, 604
  - Yellow, 743
  - Light Yellow 744,
- Size 24 embroidery needle
- 20x20cm (8x8in) piece of 14 count white aida fabric

* Mix and match these threads to match your own skin tone, hair shade and outfit colour of choice. I chose Mahogany (301) and Tan Light (738) to match me but I'd love to see how you interpret the colours to include yourself in the hoop.

Strands: For this design, use two strands of thread for cross stitch (or one if using the loop method) and one for backstitch.

How to Stitch

1. I started stitching this hoop by adding the girl (AKA me) starting with the hair as this was closest to the centre of the hoop and pattern.

2. I then stitched the text and moved on to the bubbles, stitching them one by one around the hoop.

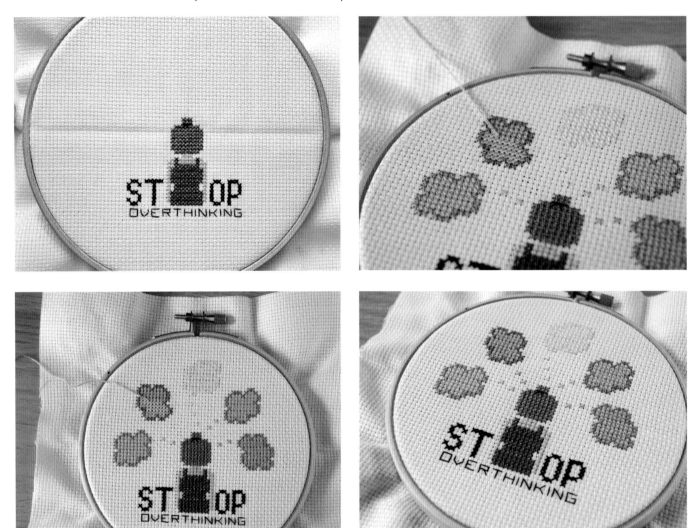

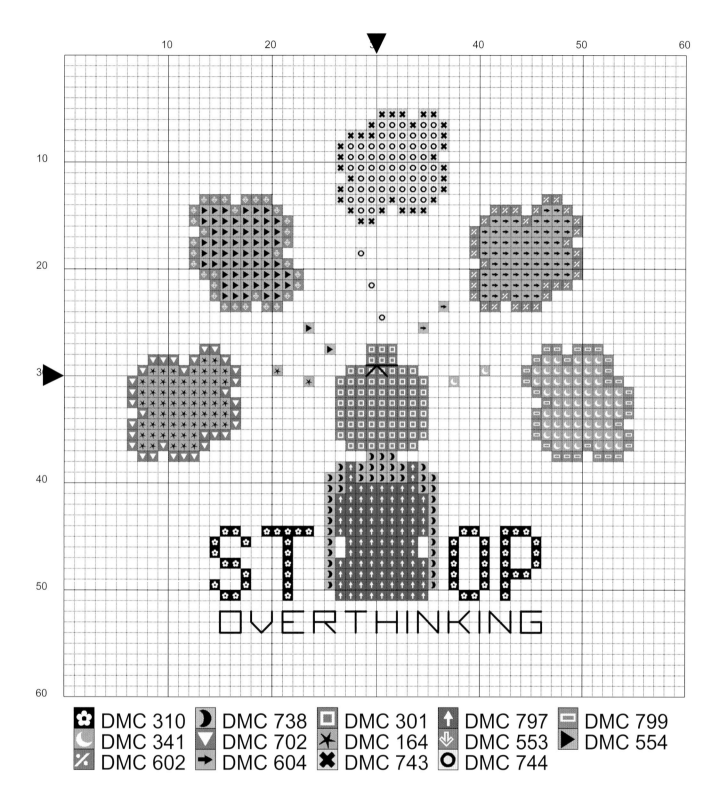

✿ DMC 310	☽ DMC 738	▢ DMC 301	↑ DMC 797	⊟ DMC 799
☾ DMC 341	▽ DMC 702	✶ DMC 164	⬇ DMC 553	▶ DMC 554
⁒ DMC 602	➜ DMC 604	✖ DMC 743	○ DMC 744	

What this project means to me

Often when life gets too busy, I feel like my brain turns to mush. It is because I am trying to spread my attention on too many things at the same time. The balance between mum, wife and creative business owner can be difficult sometimes, and when my brain starts getting foggy, I know I've split my focus too much.

I'm still working on finding that better balance, but the first change I usually make when the fog hits is to remove my mobile phone from the equation. When I have too many plates spinning, social media and general phone stuff can become really consuming. More recently I've been using the Do Not Disturb feature on my phone. I have amended the settings to allow phone calls and messages so I can be contactable, but it removes notifications for everything else, specifically emails and Instagram. It's only a small change, but it allows me to fully focus on what I need to, when I need to.

What action could you take that would allow you to have more focus and keep your mind healthy?

Materials
- 13cm (5in) embroidery hoop for stitching
- DMC embroidery thread in the following shades:
  - Black, 310
  - Green, 702
  - Light Green, 164
  - Purple, 209
- Size 24 embroidery needle
- 20x20cm (8x8in) piece of 14 count white aida fabric

Strands: For this design, use two strands of thread for cross stitch (or one if using the loop method) and one for backstitch.

How to Stitch

1. To stitch this project, I started with the word Focus in the centre of the hoop.

2. I then added the purple shadow effect stitches and worked my way out to the florals and backstitched text at the top,

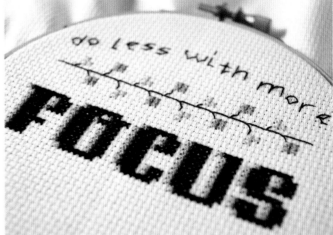

3. and bottom.

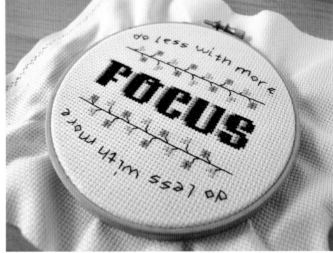

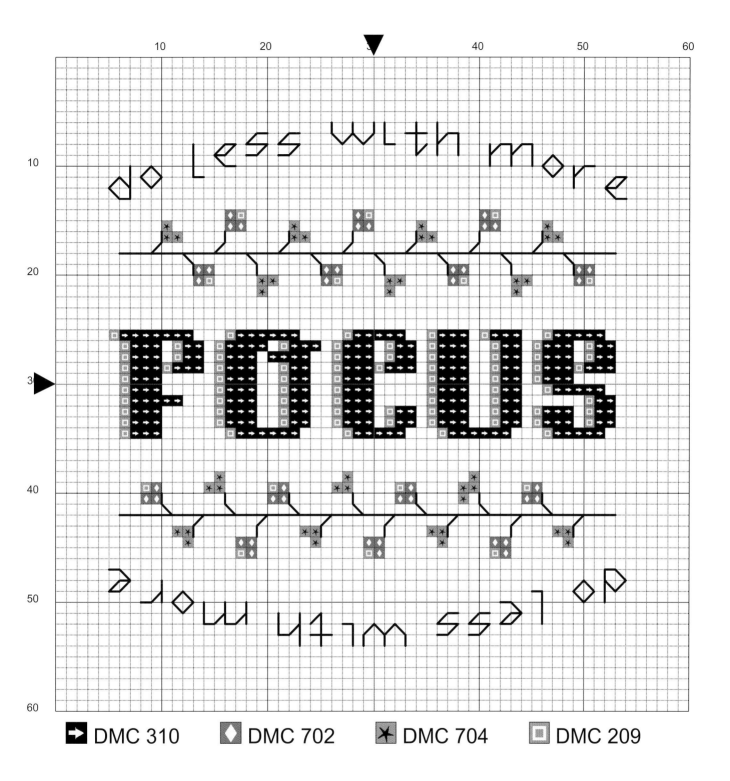

DMC 310 ◆ **DMC 702** ✳ **DMC 704** ▣ **DMC 209**

It feels important to end the book with a message that sums up the overall project themes. Taking a moment to meditate is something that we can all benefit from. Whether you need to learn to rest (page 33), let yourself bloom (page 82) or unwind and relax (page 105), taking time to intentionally live in the moment will help you to achieve the calm that you sometimes crave.

For this project, I chose cooling shades of purple and blue to bring a calming energy to the design, with clouds representing our thoughts as they slowly float away in the sky. Similarly, like these clouds, I hope you will also float away from this book feeling empowered and motivated, with a selection of mindful messages to help you travel along your own cross-stitching journey.

Materials

- 15cm (6in) snap frame for stitching
- DMC embroidery thread in the following shades:
  - Black, 310
  - Lavender, 209
  - Light Lavender, 211
  - Blue, 799
  - Light Blue, 341
  - White, BLANC
- Size 24 embroidery needle
- 23x23cm (9in) piece of 14 count white aida fabric

Strands: For this design, use two strands of thread for cross stitch (or one if using the loop method) and one for backstitch.

How to Stitch

1. For this pattern I started by stitching the black text in the centre of the design, along with the black lines top and bottom.

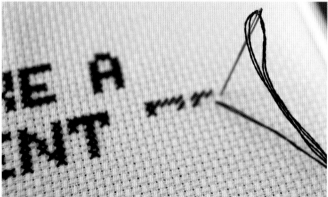

2. I then added the clouds and finished the project by adding the lighter-coloured swirls around the clouds.

➡️ DMC 310   ▷ DMC 209   ♥ DMC 211   ✖ DMC 799   ◉ DMC 341
◈ DMC BLANC

CHAPTER EIGHT

WAYS TO FINISH YOUR CROSS STITCH

There are lots of different ways you can finish your cross stitch, here are some of my favourite methods to finish a project:

HOW TO FINISH YOUR EMBROIDERY HOOP: METHOD ONE

You will need

- Cotton fabric to decorate the back of your hoop, this can be patterned or plain
- Scissors
- Needle
- Thread

Step 1 Unscrew your hoop and remove the aida.

Step 2 Cut a piece of cotton fabric. This can be patterned or plain to complement your stitching and will be used to cover up the stitches on the back of your aida.

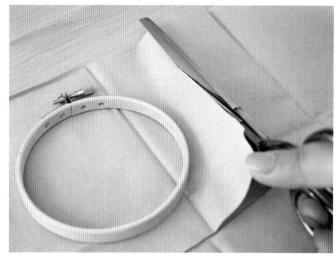

Step 3 On a clean surface, lay the inner hoop, followed by the cotton fabric (face down if it's patterned) and your aida (stitches face up).

Place your outer hoop on top and sandwich the two pieces of fabric into the hoop.

The cotton fabric will cover the back of your stitching, so this is a great method if you've stitched something as a gift.

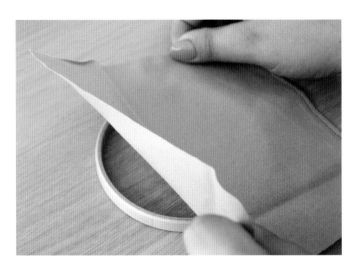

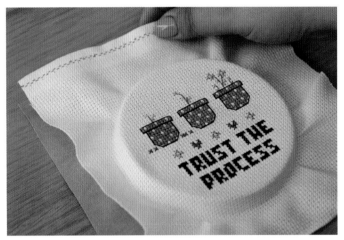

Step 4 Pull the fabric into place and then tighten the screw at the top of your hoop as much as you can.

Step 5 Trim the cotton fabric closely to the hoop.

Step 6 Trim the excess aida fabric to approximately one inch around the diameter of your hoop.

Step 7 Leaving a tail of thread behind, run a stitch along the outside of this excess aida fabric.

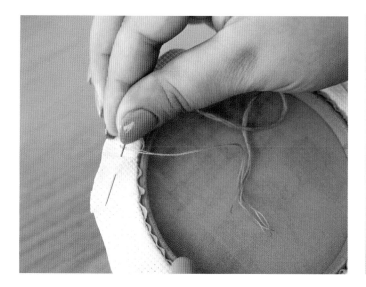
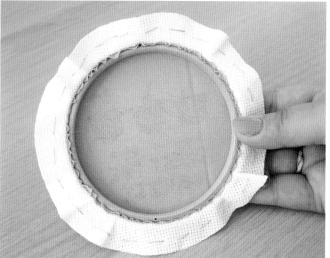

Step 8 Pull gently on the two ends of thread until all of the excess fabric has gathered together, then tie these pieces together to hold the fabric in place.

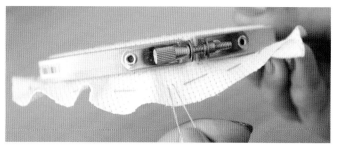

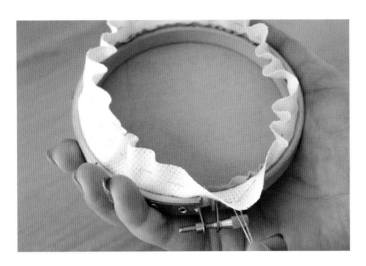
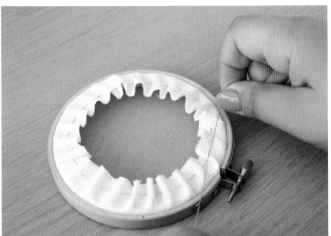

This will securely tuck the excess aida fabric behind your hoop and out of sight from the front.

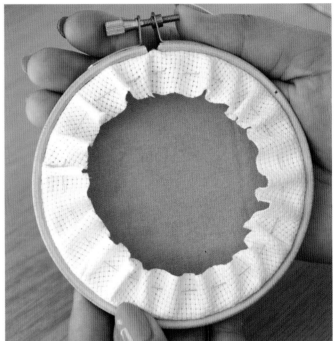

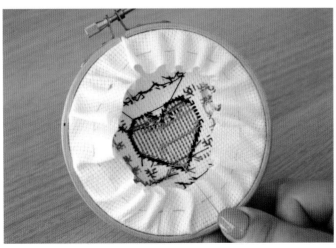

TIP You can also use this method without the additional fabric to cover the reverse side of your stitching.

HOW TO FINISH YOUR EMBROIDERY HOOP: METHOD TWO

You will need

- Cotton fabric to decorate the back of your hoop, this can be patterned or plain
- Scissors
- Super Glue

Follow Steps 1-4 of Method One:

 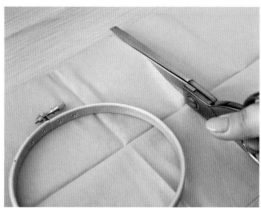 

Step 5 Trim the excess fabric (both the cotton fabric and aida) around your hoop as closely to the hoop as you can. I used fabric scissors to trim roughly around the hoop and then smaller embroidery scissors to tidy.

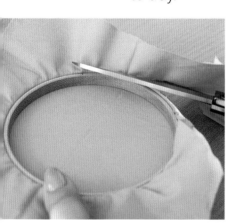  

Step 6 To secure the fabric in place and avoid any loose fabric fraying from the back of your hoop, I added some dabs of super glue.

Following the instructions on your bottle, carefully dab the super glue around the back of your hoop, where the small trim of fabric remains.

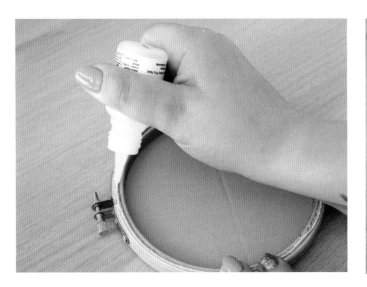 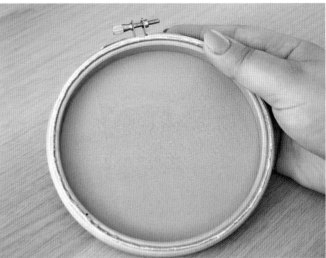

 TIP As with method one, you can use this method without the additional cotton fabric, if you would prefer to leave the back of your stitching visible.

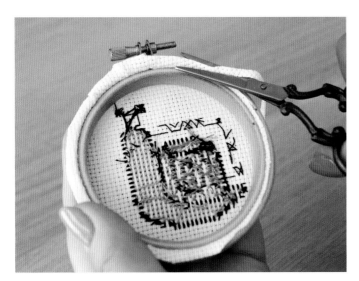 

HOW TO MOUNT YOUR CROSS STITCH

Mounting is an alternative method to finishing your cross-stitch project and is great if you prefer not to use an embroidery hoop or wish to display your stitching in a different way.

You will need:
- 5mm Foamboard (I purchased mine from Hobbycraft in A4 sheets)
- Scissors
- Pencil
- Glass headed pins (I have used 0.6mm x 30mm) in colours that match or complement your stitching
- Ruler

Step 1 Locate the centre of your cross stitch and mark on the reverse side with a pencil. Measure out from the centre point and mark the size you would like your foamboard. For this example, A Moment to Meditate, I have marked 3 inches from the centre with the intention of mounting it on to a 6x6in piece of foamboard.

Step 2 Measure out the size of foamboard you will need for the project, I cut mine down to a 6-inch square. To cut, score along your lines with scissors or a blade.

 TIP If your foamboard edges are rough you could give them a quick (and gentle) sand at this point.

Step 3 Lay your foamboard on to the reverse of your stitching, lining it up with the marks you made in step one.

Step 4 Fold over the edges of your fabric and hold in place using one pin on each edge. Then proceed to add an additional two pins on each side to secure.

Step 5 Tape in the sides of fabric, using masking tape to hold in place.

Step 6 Fold in the corners then tape down any remaining fabric

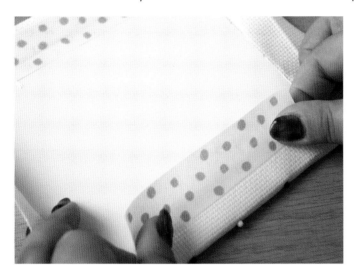 

Step 7 Add an additional two pins along the top and bottom to ensure the fabric is held in place securely. This will also ensure that the cross stitch will stand level if propped up on a shelf (for example).

TIP If your tape is strong and secure, you may wish to remove the pins once the cross stitch has been mounted. I chose pins that complemented the cross stitch so left them in to finish the piece.

A SHORT RECAP

Firstly, I'd like to thank you from the bottom of my heart for taking the time to read my book. It has truly been a labour of love. More than anything, I wanted the book to be more than just a collection of patterns. By sharing my own experiences and honest reflections on life I hope that you will have the confidence to seek out help if it's needed and use the projects and exercises within this book to reflect and enlighten your mind.

Through the combination of Mini Mindful Stitches, Positive Affirmations, Mindful Messages and Self-Care Stitches, I hope that you've gained a greater sense of the importance of slowing down and appreciating all that you have, especially the little things that can sometimes go unnoticed.

RESOURCES

Sew Sophie Crafts is my website and home to all of my cross-stitch kits, stitching accessories and quarterly subscription box: www.sewsophiecrafts.co.uk

Follow me on social media @sewsophiecrafts to stay up to date with all things Sew Sophie, including special offers and new releases.

Moving Mindset Hypnotherapy has made such a positive impact on my own mindset. Amy has been a huge help, not only through my own wellness journey but by providing insightful information to support this book too. You can find more about Amy here: www.movingmindset.co.uk

Mind have some excellent resources. Not only do they provide mental health support, they also have a wealth of information on mindful activities on their website too: www.mind.org.uk

The Mindfulness Project is a not-for-profit online hub that provides an extensive programme of mindfulness meditation courses, events and therapy. You can also read its many insightful blogs here: https://www.londonmindful.com/

The Cross Stitch Creatives is a community platform on Instagram that I run alongside some other fantastic small businesses. The page is set up to regularly share and promote businesses within the stitching community, along with top tips and tutorials to help beginners find their way into stitching too. You can find us here: @crossstitchcreatives

I've also mentioned a few other small-business friends throughout the book. Here are links to their independent websites, please have a browse:
- Iris folding kits and mesmerising tutorials www.prettyinpaperbyb.com
- Cross Stitch and Embroidery for 'people who give a stitch' www.hellotreaclestore.com
- Modern embroidery and workshops www.pixelsandpurls.co.uk
- Joyful embroidery projects and lots of colour www.hellohooray.com
- Chunky and funky needlework kits www.titchstitchuk.etsy.com

ACKNOWLEDGEMENTS

I'd like to thank everyone who has encouraged and supported me through my journey into authorhood. I am positive that I would not have coped without the continuous motivation from my husband Dan – thank you for always pushing me to be the very best version of myself and gently reminding me to snap out of it when I have a wobble. Along with my parents, in-laws and closest friends for your kind support, even when I felt like I'd bitten off more than I could chew (or a word count more than I could comprehend).

I wouldn't have found the confidence to write this without the wonderful volunteers who came forward to share their stories. Thank you for your vulnerability and for trusting me with honest accounts of your own well-being journeys. With an extra thanks to Imogen, Alison and Naomi for allowing me to share some of your quotes within in the book.

Thank you to Amy Odd for guiding me on my journey to becoming a more confident and authentic version of me, and for your expertise and support with the book. And to Amy Louise Photography for providing the most excellent headshots and brand photography.

Lastly, but by no means least, thank you to my publishers White Owl Books (Imprint of Pen & Sword) for believing in my vision for *Sew Mindful Cross Stitch* and for helping me bring my book dreams to life.